Learning Raspberry Pi

Unlock your creative programming potential by creating
web technologies, image processing, electronics- and
robotics-based projects using the Raspberry Pi

Samarth Shah

[PACKT] open source✳
PUBLISHING community experience distilled

BIRMINGHAM - MUMBAI

Learning Raspberry Pi

First published: April 2015

Production reference: 1200415

Published by Packt Publishing Ltd.
Livery Place
35 Livery Street
Birmingham B3 2PB, UK.

ISBN 978-1-78398-282-0

www.packtpub.com

Credits

Author
Samarth Shah

Reviewers
Bill Van Besien
Gary Woodfine
Werner Ziegelwanger, MSc

Commissioning Editor
Julian Ursell

Acquisition Editors
Richard Harvey
Aaron Lazar

Content Development Editor
Ruchita Bhansali

Technical Editor
Vijin Boricha

Copy Editor
Janbal Dharmaraj

Project Coordinator
Kranti Berde

Proofreaders
Ting Baker
Paul Hindle

Indexer
Hemangini Bari

Graphics
Disha Haria
Abhinash Sahu

Production Coordinator
Melwyn D'sa

Cover Work
Melwyn D'sa

About the Author

Samarth Shah is an electronics engineer who loves to explore cutting-edge hardware as well as software technologies. Currently, he is working at User Experience Group, R&D wing, Infosys Limited. He has given talks at various national as well as international conferences. He also writes technical articles for various electronics and open source magazines. In his spare time , he writes non-technical blogs at `http://shahsamarth.wordpress.com`.

I would like to thank my parents, Pareshbhai and Sandhyaben, for their constant encouragement. Special thanks to my brother, Utsav, for his continuous support.

About the Reviewers

Bill Van Besien is a software engineer whose work has primarily been in the realm of spacecraft flight software architecture, UAV autonomy software, and cyber security pertaining to space mission operations. Over the past several years, he has developed software and served on the mission operations team for several NASA space missions. He holds MS and BS degrees in computer science, with a focus on cryptography and computer security. Bill splits his time between the spacecraft flight software group at the Johns Hopkins University Applied Physics Lab and Nextility, a solar energy start-up in Washington, DC. You can find more information about his projects at `http://billvb.github.io`.

Werner Ziegelwanger, MSc has studied game engineering and simulation and got his master's degree in 2011. His master's thesis was published with the title *Terrain Rendering with Geometry Clipmaps for Games*, published by Diplomica Verlag. His hobbies include programming, games, and all kinds of technical gadgets.

Werner worked as a self-employed programmer for some years and mainly did web projects. At that time, he started his own blog (`http://developer-blog.net`), which is about the Raspberry Pi, Linux, and open source.

Since 2013, Werner has been working as a Magento developer and head of programming at mStage GmbH, an eCommerce company focused on Magento.

www.PacktPub.com

Support files, eBooks, discount offers, and more

For support files and downloads related to your book, please visit www.PacktPub.com.

Did you know that Packt offers eBook versions of every book published, with PDF and ePub files available? You can upgrade to the eBook version at www.PacktPub.com and as a print book customer, you are entitled to a discount on the eBook copy. Get in touch with us at service@packtpub.com for more details.

At www.PacktPub.com, you can also read a collection of free technical articles, sign up for a range of free newsletters and receive exclusive discounts and offers on Packt books and eBooks.

https://www2.packtpub.com/books/subscription/packtlib

Do you need instant solutions to your IT questions? PacktLib is Packt's online digital book library. Here, you can search, access, and read Packt's entire library of books.

Why subscribe?

- Fully searchable across every book published by Packt
- Copy and paste, print, and bookmark content
- On demand and accessible via a web browser

Free access for Packt account holders

If you have an account with Packt at www.PacktPub.com, you can use this to access PacktLib today and view 9 entirely free books. Simply use your login credentials for immediate access.

Table of Contents

Preface

The Raspberry Pi is an affordable, credit card-sized computer developed by the Raspberry Pi Foundation as a response to the decline in the number of applicants for computer science courses at the University of Cambridge. Eben Upton, the founder of the Raspberry Pi Foundation, believes that the current generation of children do not have as many opportunities to discover their interests in programming as his did. His generation grew up with computers such as the BBC Micro, Commodore 64, and the ZX Spectrum, all of which booted into a programming environment. The current generation of devices, on the other hand, is geared towards consuming content, rather than creating it. Although the Raspberry Pi makes an excellent home theater computer and retro gaming device, it is primarily designed to be a tool to learn programming. For this reason, the Foundation provides a version of the Raspbian operating system with preinstalled development tools and learning material, making it easy to get started.

When the Raspberry Pi was launched, it showed itself to be more popular than the designers could have imagined as the ten thousand units that were manufactured were sold out within minutes and the distributor websites were brought down by the unexpected load on their servers. In the first year, the Raspberry Pi Foundation has sold over a million units and attracted a community of hackers and makers passionate about teaching and learning. This includes the official forum (accessible at http://www.raspberrypi.org/forums/), where you can ask questions or share your project; the IRC channel on Freenode, where you can chat and get live support; the wiki hosted by eLinux (accessible at http://elinux.org/RPi_Hub), where you can find tutorials; and all the information you need to get started and the plethora of other websites dedicated to add-ons and accessories for the Raspberry Pi.

The Raspberry Pi may seem like a replacement for a low-end desktop, and the powerful GPU makes it a handy media center capable of playing HD videos. However, its true value comes from its flexibility. The General Purpose Input/Output (GPIO) pins allow the Raspberry Pi to be used for a wide variety of applications. Home automation, weather stations, industrial control, robotics, arcade gaming cabinets, and quadcopters are just some of the possibilities.

As a constant stream of exciting projects built around the Raspberry Pi surfaces all over the Internet, you may find yourself getting interested in seeing what you can do with your Raspberry Pi. This book aims to provide all of the tools you will need to turn an idea into a working prototype.

What this book covers

Chapter 1, Getting Started with Raspberry Pi, teaches you about different operating systems, alternative installation methods, and how to set up your own web server running WordPress.

Chapter 2, Developing Web Applications, takes you into HTML, CSS, JavaScript, and Python and teaches you to develop your own web application to stream music from your Raspberry Pi anywhere in the world.

Chapter 3, Introduction to Electronics, teaches everything you need to get started with electronics, even if you have not touched a soldering iron before. This chapter provides an introduction to the laws of electronics to basic components, common circuits, and prototyping methods. In this chapter, you will learn how to build a math alarm clock with an e-mail notification.

Chapter 4, Getting into Robotics, introduces you to building a remote-controlled rover, capable of driving around within the Wi-Fi coverage and streaming back videos and sensor data.

Chapter 5, Introduction to Image Processing, takes you into the world of image processing, understand the basics. After developing a time-lapse video using the Raspberry Pi camera, you will learn to build a Twitter-controlled Raspberry Pi camera.

Chapter 6, Image Processing Algorithms, introduces you to image processing algorithms. This chapter will also teach you to build and run widely run machine learning examples such as object detection and face detection.

Chapter 7, Troubleshooting, Tips/Tricks, and Resources for Advanced Users, solves common problems and shows ways the Raspberry Pi can be modified to make it more robust and stable. Find out why some SD cards do not work and how to make them work, why the Raspberry Pi resets when certain USB devices are plugged in, and how to make it an issue of the past.

What you need for this book

Throughout this book, it is assumed that you have a Raspberry Pi with the required peripherals and that you are able to install and boot an operating system using NOOBS or RAW images. Additionally, you should have some exposure to Linux and familiarity with general programming concepts. The later chapters deal with electronics, and to get the most out of them, you will need to acquire some common components.

Who this book is for

This book is written for computer literate adults coming from a Linux, PC, or Mac desktop and wishing to learn how to create things with the Raspberry Pi. The book does not dwell on easily accessible information, but does not assume expert knowledge in any particular field either. Thus, it is accessible and engaging to anyone interested in the Raspberry Pi.

Conventions

In this book, you will find a number of text styles that distinguish between different kinds of information. Here are some examples of these styles and an explanation of their meaning.

Code words in text, database table names, folder names, filenames, file extensions, pathnames, dummy URLs, user input, and Twitter handles are shown as follows: "Now, type `startx` to load the familiar UI."

A block of code is set as follows:

```
<!DOCTYPE html>
<html lang="en">
<head>
  <meta charset="UTF-8">
  <title>Hello world</title>
</head>
```

When we wish to draw your attention to a particular part of a code block, the relevant lines or items are set in bold:

```
def fileclick(req):
  if 'id' not in req.form:
return listloc(session['currdir'])
  clickedfile = safe_join(session['currdir'], req.form['id'])
if path.isfile(clickedfile):
    clickedfile = url_for('static',
    filename = clickedfile.replace(app.static_folder+'/',''))
return clickedfile
  return 0
```

Any command-line input or output is written as follows:

```
# dd if=file.img of=/dev/mmcblk0 bs=4M
```

New terms and **important words** are shown in bold. Words that you see on the screen, for example, in menus or dialog boxes, appear in the text like this: "Finally, click **Write** and remove the card."

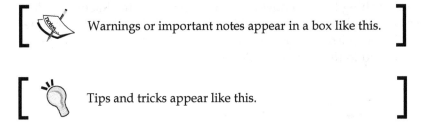

Warnings or important notes appear in a box like this.

Tips and tricks appear like this.

Reader feedback

Feedback from our readers is always welcome. Let us know what you think about this book—what you liked or disliked. Reader feedback is important for us as it helps us develop titles that you will really get the most out of.

To send us general feedback, simply e-mail feedback@packtpub.com, and mention the book's title in the subject of your message.

If there is a topic that you have expertise in and you are interested in either writing or contributing to a book, see our author guide at www.packtpub.com/authors.

Customer support

Now that you are the proud owner of a Packt book, we have a number of things to help you to get the most from your purchase.

Downloading the example code

You can download the example code files from your account at http://www. packtpub.com for all the Packt Publishing books you have purchased. If you purchased this book elsewhere, you can visit http://www.packtpub.com/support and register to have the files e-mailed directly to you.

Downloading the color images of this book

We also provide you with a PDF file that has color images of the screenshots/ diagrams used in this book. The color images will help you better understand the changes in the output. You can download this file from: https://www.packtpub. com/sites/default/files/downloads/2820OS_GraphicBundle.pdf.

Errata

Although we have taken every care to ensure the accuracy of our content, mistakes do happen. If you find a mistake in one of our books—maybe a mistake in the text or the code—we would be grateful if you could report this to us. By doing so, you can save other readers from frustration and help us improve subsequent versions of this book. If you find any errata, please report them by visiting http://www.packtpub. com/submit-errata, selecting your book, clicking on the **Errata Submission Form** link, and entering the details of your errata. Once your errata are verified, your submission will be accepted and the errata will be uploaded to our website or added to any list of existing errata under the Errata section of that title.

To view the previously submitted errata, go to https://www.packtpub.com/books/ content/support and enter the name of the book in the search field. The required information will appear under the **Errata** section.

Piracy

Piracy of copyrighted material on the Internet is an ongoing problem across all media. At Packt, we take the protection of our copyright and licenses very seriously. If you come across any illegal copies of our works in any form on the Internet, please provide us with the location address or website name immediately so that we can pursue a remedy.

Please contact us at copyright@packtpub.com with a link to the suspected pirated material.

We appreciate your help in protecting our authors and our ability to bring you valuable content.

Questions

If you have a problem with any aspect of this book, you can contact us at questions@packtpub.com, and we will do our best to address the problem.

1
Getting Started with Raspberry Pi

As you know, Raspberry Pi is a credit card computer developed by Raspberry Pi Foundation in the UK with the intention of promoting the teaching of basic computer science in schools. However, today it is used widely in all areas, including in the process of making super computer and advanced robotics operations. In this chapter, you will be introduced to Raspberry Pi and its components. As Raspberry Pi is supported by a wide variety of operating systems, this chapter provides an overview of what is available and the different installation methods. Before setting up a web server, the security implications and remote access methods are covered. Once the web server is set up and manageable remotely, it is put to use by adding WordPress. We will cover the following sections in this chapter:

- Getting to know your Raspberry Pi
- Different types of operating systems
- Installation methods
- User management
- Remotely accessing Raspberry Pi
- Installing a web server with PHP support

Getting to know your Raspberry Pi

Before you start reading further, you should know what exactly Raspberry Pi is and how you can connect different peripherals such as a keyboard and mouse to Raspberry Pi. There are several models of Raspberry Pi. The following table shows an important comparison between all the Raspberry Pi boards released as of February, 2015:

	Model A	Model A+	Model B	Model B+	Generation 2
Price	25 USD	20 USD	35 USD	35 USD	35 USD
System on Chip	Broadcom 2835	Broadcom 2835	Broadcom 2835	Broadcom 2835	Broadcom 2836
Memory	256 MB	256 MB	512 MB	512 MB	1 GB
USB 2.0 Ports	1	1	2	4	4
Onboard Network	None	None	10/100 Mbits/s Ethernet	10/100 Mbits/s Ethernet	10/100 Mbits/s Ethernet
Power Ratings	300 mA(1.5 W)	200 mA(1W)	700 mA(3.5 W)	600 mA(3.0 W)	900 mA(4.5 W)

As mentioned in the preceding table, there are variants of the model that you choose. For example in this book, Model B is used. All the code that is developed is compatible with Model B+ and Generation 2 boards. So, you can buy any of the Model B , Model B+, or even generation 2 to get the best out of this book.

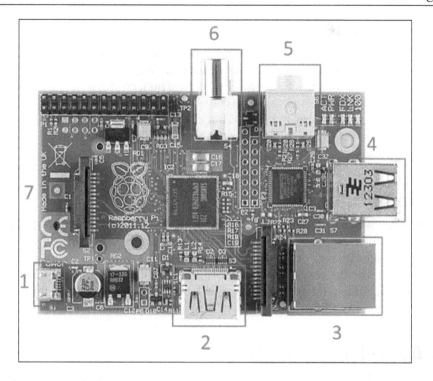

1. The microUSB power port

2. HDMI out

3. The Ethernet port

4. Dual USB 2.0 ports

5. Audio out

6. RCA video out

7. The SD card slot (back side)

Raspberry Pi supports almost all keyboards and mice; however, you can check out verified peripherals by the Raspberry Pi community at http://elinux.org/RPi_VerifiedPeripherals.

You need to load the operating system to the SD card before you start your exploration of Raspberry Pi. The following two sections have useful information about different operating systems that are supported on Raspberry Pi and on how to install particular operating systems.

Different types of operating systems

On a personal note, if you would like to dive in as quickly as possible, I would recommend visiting the official quick start guide at http://www.raspberrypi.org/ quick-start-guide in order to install Raspbian. Then, continue from the *Remotely accessing Raspberry Pi* section of this chapter. Although you will be using Raspbian throughout this book, it helps to know what else is available and how the various operating systems differ. I encourage you to try all of the available operating systems and find what suits your needs.

The Raspbian OS

Raspbian is a Linux distribution based on Debian, with all packages compiled specifically for the Raspberry Pi. Although it is a separate project, Raspberry Pi Foundation creates images of Raspbian and maintains a repository containing additional software. Because Raspbian should be familiar to Ubuntu and Linux Mint users, as it aims to be user friendly and has the largest user base; this is often the recommended distribution.

The Arch Linux ARM OS

The Arch Linux ARM OS, which is a port of Arch Linux, is also optimized for the Raspberry Pi. However, this has a different design philosophy to Raspbian. Rather than aiming to be user-friendly, Arch Linux ARM gives the user a complete control over the system. This means that instead of a distribution that just works, you have a starting point from which to build up the distribution tailored to your needs. While this may be intimidating to some newcomers, the ArchWiki (http://wiki. archlinux.org) contains perhaps the most comprehensive documentation of any distribution, making it easy to get started. The other major difference is that Arch uses the latest software. While stability may be a concern, the advantage of bleeding edge software is that you rarely have to compile from the source to get the latest features and bug fixes. Arch is the ideal distribution for users who know how they want their system to work, who are willing to spend some time getting things up and running and don't mind the occasional hiccup.

Pidora is the Raspberry Pi-optimized remix of Fedora. This is the first distribution created specifically for the Raspberry Pi and was the officially recommended distribution prior to Raspbian. Since this is an RPM-based distribution, it should be most familiar to OpenSUSE and CentOS users. Fedora attempts to avoid non-free software where possible, so things such as MP3 support and Oracle's Java are not included. Its target audience is computer literate tinkerers who are likely to contribute to the project. Although Fedora has a significant user base, Pidora itself is a minor distribution on the Raspberry Pi and is not as actively maintained as Raspbian or Arch. Therefore, getting support may be difficult in some cases.

The RISC OS

RISC OS is not related to Linux and does not share the Unix lineage. It dates back to 1987 and has not followed development in the same direction as modern operating systems. As a result, it takes a while to get used to this system, since the user interface is quite different from what most people are familiar with. It lacks the level of hardware support that Linux has, so USB devices such as Wi-Fi sticks are not supported. On the other hand, it is extremely fast and excellent for low-level programming. While Linux competes for resources with your applications, RISC OS can get out of your way and let your code have complete control over the hardware. This is a great advantage for time-sensitive tasks and applications where you want to be close to the hardware. The RISC OS website (which you can access at `http://www.riscosopen.org`) has the resources necessary to get started.

OpenELEC and Raspbmc

These two distributions are centered on XBMC, which is a media player that can turn your Raspberry Pi into a **home theater PC (HTPC)**. The major difference between the two is that **OpenELEC** is built from scratch and is designed only to be a HTPC distribution. **Raspbmc**, on the other hand, is built from Raspbian and can also be used as a general purpose distribution. Each has its own advantages and disadvantages and the final choice between the two comes down to preference. If you plan to use Raspberry Pi for specific purpose (home theater), then choose OpenELEC over Raspbmc. However, if you plan to do some general purpose stuff as well, then choose Raspbmc.

Other operating systems

Apart from the operating systems covered previously, there are many more to explore (you can access them via http://elinux.org/RPi_Distributions). These include BSD, the customized versions of Raspbian, Slackware, Gentoo, DexOS, Plan 9, and many others.

 In the remaining chapters of this book, projects are developed using Raspbian OS distribution, which is officially recommended by the Raspberry Pi Foundation.

Command summary

Although Linux distributions are quite different in their design philosophies, they are quite similar once the difference between the Init and package management systems is grasped. The important differences are summarized in the following table:

	Raspbian	Arch	Pidora
Search for software	apt-cache search <keyword>	pacman -Ss <keyword>	yum search <keyword>
Install software	apt-get install <package>	pacman -S <package>	yum install <package>
Update package index	apt-get update	pacman -Sy	yum check-update
Update packages	apt-get dist-upgrade	pacman -Syu	yum distro-sync
Remove software	apt-get remove <package>	pacman -Rc <package>	yum remove <package>
Start service	service <name> start	systemctl start <name>	systemctl start <name>
Enable service	update-rc.d <name> enable	systemctl enable <name>	systemctl enable <name>
Init system	SysVInit	systemd	systemd
Package management	APT	pacman	RPM

Installation methods

In this section, you will learn how to install an operating system to the Raspberry Pi. There are different ways using which you can install OS to Raspberry Pi. Raspberry Pi runs from the OS installed on the SD card.

 Make sure you are using the Class-10 SD card as other Class-4 cards has lots of write failure. Using the Class-10 memory card, you will have a better reading and writing experience.

NOOBS and BerryBoot

New Out Of the Box Software (NOOBS) is the official installation method developed by the Raspberry Pi Foundation as an attempt to simplify the installation procedure for beginners and add support for multiple operating systems on the same card. BerryBoot predates NOOBS and it has the advantage that it supports more operating systems, is able to install them to a USB stick, and can back up, restore, and clone operating systems.

The steps to install BerryBoot and NOOBS are as follows:

1. First, download BerryBoot at `http://www.berryterminal.com/doku.php/berryboot` or NOOBS from `http://www.raspberrypi.org/downloads`.
2. Next, format the SD card as FAT32, depending on your OS system.
3. Windows users are recommended to use SD Association's SD Formatter, which can be accessed at `https://www.sdcard.org/downloads/formatter_4/`.
4. Linux users can use GParted.
5. Then, extract the downloaded archive onto the SD card.
6. After this, the card can be ejected and inserted into the Raspberry Pi.

7. Finally, boot up the Raspberry Pi with the card inserted and follow the on-screen instructions.

 Common pitfalls include extracting into a subdirectory and incorrectly formatting the card by using a card that is too small. Although 4 GB is the recommended minimum, an installed NOOBS Raspbian requires a little more to function correctly.

Installing Raspbian using RAW images

Installing Raspbian using RAW images is the original method that was used to install an operating system onto the SD card. The RAW image contains the binary data directly as it will appear on the card. This includes the **Master Boot Record** (**MBR**) and all of the partitions. This method has clear advantages as it is supported by all the operating systems, and there is very little that can go wrong. This does not require the user to partition or format the card as everything is already contained in the image file.

There are also some disadvantages. Since the sizes of SD card vary and the image file contains a static partition table and filesystem, you will end up with unusable free space. The other problem is the lack of flexibility. The image files make it hard to boot multiple operating systems from the same card or have an operating system on the SD card.

Writing an image using Windows

1. First, download Win32 Disk Imager from `https://launchpad.net/win32-image-writer`.

2. Next, select the appropriate image file.

3. Then, select the SD card from the drop-down menu.

4. Finally, click **Write** and remove the card.

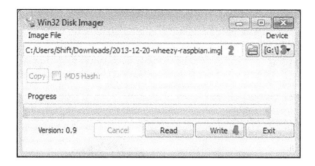

The annotations in the preceding screenshot of **Win32 Disk Imager** correspond to the previous step numbers

Writing an image using Linux

1. First, ensure the card is not mounted.

2. Then write to disk, replacing mmcblk0 with the appropriate device. You can do this by running the following command:

```
# dd if=file.img of=/dev/mmcblk0 bs=4M
```

 Make sure you are pointing to the correct partition. If you point to the main OS partition by mistake, it might corrupt your current OS.

3. Before removing the card, it is important to flush the filesystem buffers by running the following command:

```
# sync
```

 Some more common problems to look out for include removing the card before flushing the filesystem buffers, writing to a partition instead of the whole card or writing the zip file instead of the extracted image file, and so on.

Raspbian OS interface

Once you have installed the Raspbian OS to the SD card, insert the SD card into Raspberry Pi and connect the keyboard, mouse, and LCD screen using the HDMI port and power the Raspberry Pi. On the first run, it will ask for your username and to type `pi` and the password as `raspberry` when prompted. Now, type `startx` to load the familiar UI.

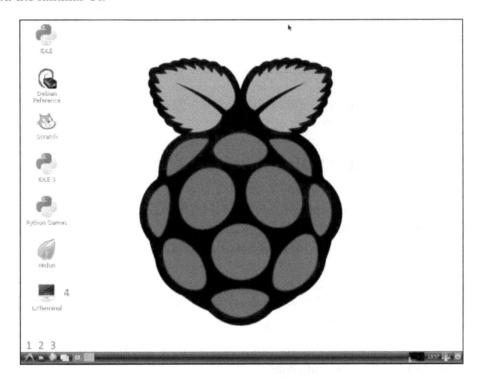

1. The Start button

2. Folders

3. The Midori browser

4. Terminal (command windows)

Now, connect the Ethernet cable to your Raspberry Pi.

Before you start reading further, I recommend you spend some time playing with the OS and trying some of the commands that you are familiar with, of the operating system (Windows, Linux, Mac) you are using right now. Some of the things you can try are:

- Find out what all applications are already installed on your Raspberry Pi
- Access your e-mail account using the Midori browser
- Get yourself familiarized with the folder structure

Expanding the filesystem

If you are using Raspbian, this can be done by choosing the **Expand Filesystem** option within the `raspi-config` script, which executes on the first boot. However, you can also launch this script manually by running `sudo raspi-config`. If your distribution does not provide an automated way to expand the filesystem and you do not have GParted available on your PC, this can be done on the Raspberry Pi itself. For this example, a card containing the Arch Linux image is resized by following these steps:

1. First, launch fdisk by typing the following command:

   ```
   # fdisk /dev/mmcblk0
   ```

2. Then, press *p*, followed by *Enter* in order to display the current partition table, which should be displayed as follows:

   ```
   Command (m for help): p
   Disk /dev/mmcblk0: 29.7 GiB, 31918653440 bytes, 62341120
   sectors
   Units: sectors of 1 * 512 = 512 bytes
   Sector size (logical/physical): 512 bytes / 512 bytes
   I/O size (minimum/optimal): 512 bytes / 512 bytes
   Disklabel type: dos
   Disk identifier: 0x417ee54b
   ```

Device	Boot	Start	End	Blocks	Id System
/dev/mmcblk0p1 (LBA)		2048	186367	92160	c W95 FAT32
/dev/mmcblk0p2		186368	3667967	1740800	5 Extended
/dev/mmcblk0p5		188416	3667967	1739776	83 Linux

3. Since the card contains an extended partition (p2) with a logical partition side of it (p5), you can simply delete partition 2, so partition 5 will be removed automatically. This can be carried out as follows:

```
Command (m for help): d
Partition number (1,2,5, default 5): 2


Partition 2 has been deleted.
```

4. After this, create a new extended partition to replace the one that has been deleted. Ensure that the first sector of the new partition matches the one deleted. Then, accept the default last sector, as it will automatically use all of the free space:

```
Command (m for help): n


Partition type:
    p    primary (1 primary, 0 extended, 3 free)
    e    extended
Select (default p): e
Partition number (2-4, default 2):
First sector (186368-62341119, default 186368):
Last sector, +sectors or +size{K,M,G,T,P} (186368-62341119,
default 62341119):


Created a new partition 2 of type 'Extended' and of size
29.7 GiB.
```

5. Then, create a new logical partition, again making sure the start sector matches the old start sector of partition 5 and accept the default last sector:

```
Command (m for help): n


Partition type:
    p    primary (1 primary, 1 extended, 2 free)
    l    logical (numbered from 5)
Select (default p): l


Adding logical partition 5
First sector (188416-62341119, default 188416):
```

```
Last sector, +sectors or +size{K,M,G,T,P} (188416-62341119,
default 62341119):
```

```
Created a new partition 5 of type 'Linux' and of size 29.7
GiB.
```

6. Next, display the partition table again to make sure that only the end sectors are different from the original partition table:

```
Command (m for help): p
```

```
Disk /dev/mmcblk0: 29.7 GiB, 31918653440 bytes, 62341120
sectors
```

```
Units: sectors of 1 * 512 = 512 bytes
```

```
Sector size (logical/physical): 512 bytes / 512 bytes
```

```
I/O size (minimum/optimal): 512 bytes / 512 bytes
```

```
Disklabel type: dos
```

```
Disk identifier: 0x417ee54b
```

Device	Boot	Start	End	Blocks	Id	System
/dev/mmcblk0p1 FAT32 (LBA)		2048	186367	92160	c	W95
/dev/mmcblk0p2 Extended		186368	62341119	31077376	5	
/dev/mmcblk0p5		188416	62341119	31076352	83	Linux

7. Once you are happy with the partition table, write it to disk and quit:

```
Command (m for help): w
```

The partition table has been altered.

8. Next, restart the Raspberry Pi by running the following command:

```
# reboot
```

9. When the Raspberry Pi has booted up, log in and resize the filesystem:

```
# resize2fs /dev/mmcblk0
```

 It is important to note that not all images have the same partition layout. You should adapt the preceding steps to suit your needs.

Installing Raspbian using raspbian-ua-netinst

Hifi's raspbian-ua-netinst is a small tool that gives you a minimal Raspbian installation, using the latest packages. This install differs greatly from the RAW image released by the Raspberry Pi Foundation and is therefore only recommended for power-users. The complete documentation can be found at `http://github.com/hifi/raspbian-ua-netinst`.

Preparing the NetInstall on Linux

The NetInstall has distributed an image, as it is simpler for Linux users. The following steps help in preparing the NetInstall on Linux:

1. First, download the installer using the following command:

   ```
   # wget http://hifi.iki.fi/raspbian-ua-netinst/raspbian-ua-netinst-latest.img.xz
   ```

2. Then, extract the image to the SD card by running this command:

   ```
   # xzcat /path/to/raspbian-ua-netinst-latest.img.xz > /dev/mmcblk0
   ```

3. Next, flush the filesystem buffers using the `sync` command.

4. Finally, remove the card, boot the Raspberry Pi, and let the installer finish.

Preparing the NetInstall on Windows

Download and extract `http://hifi.iki.fi/raspbian-ua-netinst/raspbian-ua-netinst-latest.zip` onto a FAT32 formatted SD card, as shown in the NOOBS install steps.

Post-install configuration for Raspbian distribution

The default install does not replace the kernel, customize the install to your locale, or install any of the Raspberry Pi headers and libraries. The following steps provide a more complete install:

1. First, log in as `root`, with the password `raspbian`.

2. Then, change the password using the `passwd` command.

3. If necessary, configure your locale, keyboard layout, and time zone by running the following command:

   ```
   # dpkg-reconfigure locales keyboard-configuration tzdata
   ```

4. Next, update the package index by typing this:

```
# apt-get update
```

5. Then, install the kernel, bootloader, optimized memory routines, the Raspberry Pi utilities, and a text editor by running the following command:

```
# apt-get install linux-image-rpi-rpfv raspberrypi-bootloader-
copies-and-fills libraspberrypi-bin nano
```

> The `linux-image-rpi-rpfv` package contains a kernel managed by the Raspbian project, while the `raspberrypi-bootloader` package contains a kernel provided by the Raspberry Pi Foundation. Although the Raspbian kernel is recommended, the Foundation kernel can be used instead by skipping the sixth and seventh steps.

6. The Raspbian kernel can then be installed by copying it to the boot partition using the following command:

```
# cp /vmlinuz /boot/raspbian-kernel.img
```

7. In order to avoid conflicts with the Raspberry Pi Foundation's kernel, configure the Raspberry Pi to use the new kernel. This can be done by running the following command and inserting the line `kernel raspbian-kernel.img`:

```
# nano /boot/config.txt
```

8. Finally, modify the sources list to include the `non-free` and `contrib` packages, if necessary. This includes things such as WiFi firmware, which may be required for some people. The `/etc/apt/sources.list` file should look as follows:

```
deb http://mirrordirector.raspbian.org/raspbian/ wheezy
main contrib non-free rpi
```

```
deb http://archive.raspberrypi.org/debian/ wheezy main
```

User management

Once you have Raspbian installed, it is advisable to set up a user account. The Raspberry Pi Foundation's version of Raspbian already has a user `pi`, with the password `raspberry`. A system running with the default password is not secure as the password is widely known. To avoid this problem, the password needs to be changed. The default install does not have a root password set and the user is expected to use `sudo` to run commands as root. As a result, many beginners never learn the difference between a root and a user account. This leads to misuse of `sudo` and other issues later on. A root password is set in order to allow administrative tasks to be carried out in a standard root shell and an extra user account is added to standardize the install using the following steps:

1. First, log in as `pi`.

2. Then, change the default user password by running the following command:

   ```
   # passwd
   ```

3. Next, enter a root shell by typing this:

   ```
   # sudo -i
   ```

4. Again, run `passwd` to change the password. As you are in a root shell, this will change the root password this time.

5. Add a new user with a name of your choice by entering the following command:

   ```
   # adduser steve
   ```

6. The user will not be able to carry out certain tasks without being a member of the relevant groups. The following command will add the user into the major groups:

   ```
   # usermod -a -G
   adm,dialout,cdrom,sudo,audio,video,plugdev,games,users,netdev,
   input,spi,gpio steve
   ```

 Please note that `raspi-config` is coded with the assumption that `pi` is the main user. As a result, some options (**Enable Boot to Desktop/Scratch**), will not work as expected.

If you would like to boot the desktop automatically as the new user, this can be easily accomplished without `raspi-config`:

1. First, enable the LightDM service by running this:

   ```
   # update-rc.d lightdmd enable 2
   ```

2. Set the `autologin-user` variable in `/etc/lightdm/lightdm.conf` as required. You should note that leaving it commented out with a # will present you with a login window every time you boot up, which is slightly more secure and is especially recommended if you have multiple users.

The reverse can be accomplished simply by disabling the LightDM service.

Once you installed the operating system, you can use the keyboard, mouse, and HDMI screen to get started with the development. However, many of you might not have a USB keyboard, USB mouse, and HDMI screen. In such cases, you need to access Raspberry Pi remotely.

Remotely accessing Raspberry Pi

Once the Raspberry Pi is up and running, it may be necessary to access it remotely, and there are several ways of going about it.

The SSH remote server

SSH can be used for the vast majority of remote administration tasks. It gives us full access to a remote terminal just like it is local. Because the Raspberry Pi makes a good headless server, SSH is installed and enabled by default in Raspbian. Within Linux, connecting to an SSH server is done with the `ssh` command:

```
ssh user@IP:port
```

 If you don't know how to get the IP address of Raspberry Pi, refer to *Chapter 7, Troubleshooting, Tips/Tricks, and Resources for Advanced Users, Tips and tricks* section.

The user and port parameters are optional. The username defaults to the currently logged-in user and the default port is 22.

On Windows, an SSH connection can be established using PuTTY, which you can download from `http://www.chiark.greenend.org.uk/~sgtatham/putty/`.

Securing SSH

If you want to make the Raspberry Pi accessible from outside of the local network, extra precautions should be taken to protect it from bots and hackers. Most bots simply attempt to connect on port 22 as root and brute force the password. Assuming that the password is relatively secure, this isn't a big problem, but it will eventually start filling up the logs with failed login attempts.

Changing the port number and forbidding root login over SSH is the simplest way of stopping the vast majority of automated login attempts. This can be done by editing `/etc/ssh/sshd_config` and setting the following options:

```
Port 1286 #Any unused port number is fine

PermitRootLogin no
```

 To keep things simple for the rest of the instructions, please leave the port at the default 22 for now.

However, changing the port number is not always desirable and will not stop someone from scanning for open ports. Ideally, you would disable password logins altogether and use keys. This is how it works — you generate a private and public key. The public key can be sent to a remote server. The private key, as the name implies, is kept private and is used instead of the password.

Windows users can generate the keys using the PuTTYgen tool, which is available on the PuTTY website:

1. Copy the public key to the `~/.ssh/authorized_keys` file on the Raspberry Pi (you may have to create it) and save the private key onto your PC.

2. After this, change the permissions of the `authorized_keys` file in order to protect it:

   ```
   # chmod 600 ~/.ssh/authorized_keys
   ```

3. Once this is done, you can use **Save private key** in PuTTY.

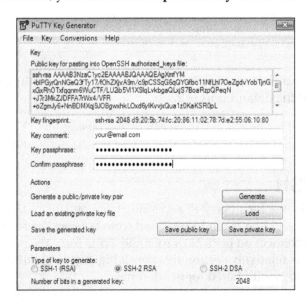

4. The following **PuTTY Key Generator** screenshot annotations show the public key to be copied and how to save the private key:

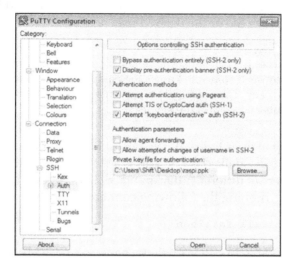

5. The highlighted area of the preceding screenshot shows how the private key can be used within PuTTY.

6. Within Linux, the keys can be generated as follows:

```
# ssh-keygen -t rsa
```

7. When prompted, accept the default save location and enter a passphrase. The content of id_rsa.pub should then be pasted into the ~/.ssh/ authorized_keys file on the Raspberry Pi. This can be done with a single command:

```
# ssh-copy-id user@IP -p PORTNUMBER
```

You should now be able to connect to the Raspberry Pi by using our private key.

8. Once you have confirmed that this works, come back to /etc/ssh/sshd_ config and disable password logins:

```
PasswordAuthentication no
```

9. You can add as many public keys to the `authorized_keys` file as necessary. For example, you may wish to allow someone else to access your Raspberry Pi. To do this, you would ask for their public keys and add it to the `authorized_keys` file of the desired user account.

 In the case the private key is stolen, it cannot be used without the passphrase. If someone knows the passphrase, it is useless without the SSH key. The combination prevents brute force connection attempts and secures the key itself.

10. The final thing to do is to install `fail2ban`. This program monitors connection attempts and bans malicious IPs. This is a very powerful tool that can be used to fight a variety of different attacks and SSH is supported by default. This can be installed by running the following command:

```
# apt-get install fail2ban
```

Open the configuration file to edit with `sudo nano /etc/fail2ban/jail.local` and paste the following content (assuming your private IP addresses are in the range 192.168.0.*):

```
# SSH
# 3 failed retry: Ban for 10 minutes
[ssh]
enabled = true
port = ssh
filter = sshd
action = iptables[name=SSH, port=ssh, protocol=tcp]
mail-whois-lines[name=%(__name__)s, dest=%(destemail)s,
logpath=%(logpath)s]
logpath = /var/log/auth.log
maxretry = 3
bantime = 600
ignoreip = 192.168.0.0/10

[ssh-ddos]
enabled = true
port = ssh
filter = sshd-ddos
action = iptables[name=SSH, port=ssh, protocol=tcp]
```

```
logpath = /var/log/auth.log
maxretry = 10
ignoreip = 192.168.0.0/10
```

Restart the `fail2ban` service:

```
sudo /etc/init.d/fail2ban restart
```

Transferring files

Besides executing commands remotely, SSH also allows us to transfer files. The `scp` command is similar to `cp`, but can copy files to and from SSH servers with the following command:

```
$ scp /path/to/src user@IP:/path/to/dst
```

This works great for a simple file transfer, but there is a more powerful command, which is as follows:

```
$ rsync /path/to/src user@IP:/path/to/dst -av
```

Rsync will only copy files that differ. By default, it does this by checking the file size and timestamp of the file, but a `-c` option can also be passed to use a checksum. This is very useful when making backups or updating source code, for example. It can also be used with a local source and destination, making it a very useful tool to get familiar with.

Windows users can use WinSCP, which is available at `http://winscp.net`. It has an excellent GUI that can use PuTTY private keys, and offers a way to move files between your PC and Raspberry Pi.

X11 Forwarding

So, you can run commands and transfer files, but what about the GUI? The X Windowing System was designed with the ability to use a remote display in mind. SSH can be used to forward remote GUI programs to the local X server. For Linux users, it's only a matter of launching SSH as before, but with the addition of a `-Y` option. When you have a SSH session ready, try launching `leafpad`. It should show up on your display.

Windows users will require an X server running. Some options are listed here:

- Xming, available at `http://sourceforge.net/projects/xming/`
- VcXsrv, available at `http://sourceforge.net/projects/vcxsrv/`
- Cygwin/X, available at `http://x.cygwin.com/`

Maintaining remote session using screen

While **screen** is not related to SSH directly, it is an incredibly powerful combination. Under normal conditions, if our connection drops and the SSH session is lost, everything that was running inside of it is terminated. This may result in a lot of hard work being lost. The screen allows us to create a session, which you can detach and re-attach as required. While detached, everything will continue to run as normal. If the connection drops, you can simply re-attach to the screen session and continue where you left off. Unfortunately, Raspbian does not come with screen preinstalled, so run the following command to install it:

```
# apt-get install screen
```

Once installed, it can be launched by running the following command:

```
# screen
```

You will receive a welcome screen, which can be dismissed by pressing *Enter* or disabling it in ~/.screenrc.

First, you'll need to learn a few key bindings to get started with screen. The default key bindings are initiated by pressing *Ctrl + a* and are completed by another key. For example, the screen session can be detached by pressing *Ctrl + a* and then *d*. Once detached, you can return back to the screen session by running the following command:

```
# screen -x
```

What if you want to run multiple applications? On a local machine, you have multiple ttyS commands or you can open many terminals windows and tabs. Starting a new SSH session for every application would be a little inconvenient. Screen has us covered here as well. *Ctrl + a+ c* will create a new window. The first window (0) is now replaced by the new window (1). To return to the first windows, the *Ctrl + a + 0* binding will work. You can have as many windows as needed and navigate them using the *Ctrl + a + 0-9* keys. Alternatively, *Ctrl + a* will bring up a list of all windows and let us switch between them using the arrows and the *Enter* key.

This short introduction only scratches the surface of what is possible with screen. It can display multiple windows at once in a split view, allowing you to have a file browser, a media player, and a network monitor running and making them visible all at once within the screen session. Multiple users can connect to the same screen session, if remote assistance is required. Screen can be configured to display a status bar with all of the windows listed and a clock, for example. It also supports start-up scripts, which can be very useful for power users.

The reverse SSH

Your Raspberry Pi could be behind a firewall with no access to port forwarding. In such a case, you can't connect directly. However, if the computer you wish to connect from is not behind a firewall and also has an SSH server running, reverse SSH can be used. From the Raspberry Pi, start SSH with the following command:

```
$ ssh -N -R 2222:localhost:22 user@IP
```

In this case, the user and IP parameters are for the computer you wish to connect from. -N means that you do not wish to run any commands. -R 2222:localhost:22 means that port 22 on localhost is going to be tunneled to port 2222 on the remote computer.

Then, from the remote computer, you can connect to localhost on port 2222 and that will redirect to port 22 on the Raspberry Pi launching SSH as follows:

```
$ ssh user@localhost -p 2222
```

The disadvantage is that this needs to be prepared in advance and will only last as long as both computers are on. This can be circumvented by preparing a script that runs every 15 minutes and creates the tunnel if it's not already established.

The other problem is that one computer must not be behind a firewall. The solution is to use a middleman server, which the Raspberry Pi will establish a tunnel with. Then, you can connect to this server and be tunneled through to the Raspberry Pi. However, the fundamental problem still remains, as now you require yet another server that is not behind a firewall. If such a server is not available, a third-party solution such as Hamachi, may be an option.

Virtual display using VNC

VNC is quite different from the other options and comes in two flavors. The first allows for the display that is attached to the Raspberry Pi to be mirrored remotely and is called **x11vnc**. One example of where this is handy is remote assistance. The other option is a **virtual display**, which is not shown on the Raspberry Pi's monitor itself. The virtual display approach is useful when you would like to be able to launch multiple, independent VNC sessions. In order to connect to a VNC server, you will need a VNC client. There are clients and servers available for all major operating systems, from Windows to Android. **TightVNC** is one example. The installation package differs from other distributions, but once installed, it can be launched using VNC Viewer.

In order to use the real display, you need to install x11vnc on the Raspberry Pi by running this:

```
# apt-get install x11vnc
```

If the X server is running, x11vnc can be launched directly by running x11vnc. By default, x11vnc will exit once the client disconnects. This can be prevented by adding the -forever option.

In order to use a virtual display, install a TightVNC server on the Raspberry Pi by running the following command:

```
# apt-get install tightvncserver
```

When running vncserver for the first time, you will be taken through a quick set up procedure.

Pay attention to the output, as it will say which display the server is running on. When connecting, specify this display as the port number.

In order to stop a running virtual VNC display, the -kill option can be used. The following command will kill the VNC server using display :1:

```
$ vncserver -kill :1
```

Share the keyboard and mouse using Synergy

Synergy is used to share the keyboard and mouse across multiple systems. For example, you can have a display connected to the Raspberry Pi and control it from the keyboard and mouse on your PC. This will be useful if you would like to use the full desktop environment without VNC, but don't have a spare keyboard, or if you would like to have a dual-display setup with one of the displays dedicated to the Raspberry Pi.

1. On the PC, download and install the synergy server, either from the official website (http://synergy-foss.org) or from your distribution's repository. Running it will guide you through a setup procedure, which will prepare it for use.

> The version of synergy in the Raspbian repository is not supported by newer servers. It is possible to download an older server (1.3.8) or compile the client for Raspbian, which will not be covered here.

2. Install Synergy on the Raspberry Pi by running this:

```
# apt-get install synergy
```

3. Finally, from the Raspberry Pi's desktop, launch the Synergy client with the following command:

```
# synergyc IP
```

Installing a web server

The first instinct may be to install Apache. However, nginx performs better on lower-end hardware. It should be noted that Apache can work just as well if the unnecessary plugins are removed and Apache is configured appropriately. For something that works fairly well out of the box, nginx is a great start.

1. First, install nginx and php with an accelerator and a MySQL server with the following command:

```
# apt-get install nginx php5-fpm php5-mysql php-apc mysql-server
```

 You will be prompted to set a password for MySQL; please make sure you remember it, as you will need it later.

2. Then, start the nginx service:

```
# service nginx start
```

3. In order to ensure nginx is working, open up a browser and connect to the Raspberry Pi's IP. You should be greeted with a **Welcome to nginx!** message.

 The configuration file for nginx is located in /etc/nginx/nginx. conf. The file then imports additional configuration files from /etc/ nginx/conf.d/*.conf and /etc/nginx/sites-enabled/*. The idea is that you store the configuration for the individual sites you want to run in the /etc/nginx/sites-available/ directory and then symlink the ones you wish to enable into the /etc/nginx/sites-enabled/ directory.

4. Next, create a configuration for our site based on the default and then enable it by running the following commands:

```
# cp /etc/nginx/sites-available/default /etc/nginx/sites-
available/pisite
```

```
# unlink /etc/nginx/sites-enabled/default
```

```
# ln -s /etc/nginx/sites-available/pisite /etc/nginx/sites-
enabled/default
```

5. After this, change the content of /etc/nginx/sites-available/pisite as follows:

```
server {

        root /srv/www;

        index index.html index.htm;

}
```

6. At this point, this is not a valid entry, as /srv/www does not exist. Create the directory and add a simple index.html by executing the following commands:

```
# mkdir /srv/www
```

```
# echo "Hello world" > /srv/www/index.html
```

7. Finally, reload the nginx configuration so that our changes take effect by running this command:

```
# service nginx reload
```

Refresh the web page to ensure the new site is properly configured.

Adding PHP support

Now that the web server is working, it is a good idea to configure it to use PHP, using the following steps:

1. First, start the php5-fpm service, which nginx will communicate with to provide PHP support using FastCGI. This can be done by running the following command:

```
# service php5-fpm start
```

2. Then, modify the pisite configuration as follows:

```
server {

        root /srv/www;

index index.php index.html index.htm;
```

```
location ~ \.php$ {
                fastcgi_pass unix:/var/run/php5-fpm.sock;
                fastcgi_index index.php;
    include fastcgi_params;
        }
    }
```

3. Next, remove the old index file by running this command:

    `# rm /srv/www/index.html`

4. Create `/srv/www/index.php` with the following content:

    ```
    <?php
            phpinfo();
    ?>
    ```

    The `<?php ... ?>` tags indicate that the contents is to be interpreted as PHP. The `phpinfo()` function is used to return configuration information.

5. Finally, reload the configuration:

    `# service nginx reload`

Refreshing the page should bring up information about your PHP configuration, indicating that PHP is working.

Now you have installed popular LAMP server on your Raspberry Pi. Web application development using the LAMP stack is the preferred option for developers to create a stable, reliable, and highly efficient application. Moreover, developing the application using LAMP stack and deploying code on LAMP stack is comparatively easy. Having installed all these stacks, you might want to host your own personal blog/website using Raspberry Pi powered by popular WordPress.

Installing WordPress

Once the server is installed, it can be used to host a personal website powered by WordPress:

1. First, download and extract WordPress to the www directory by running the following commands:

    `# wget http://wordpress.org/latest.zip`

    `# unzip latest.zip -d /srv/www/`

2. Then, launch the MySQL command-line tool. When prompted for a password, enter the password setup when installing MySQL:

```
# mysql -u root -p
```

3. Next, create a new database called `piwordpress` by entering the following command:

```
> CREATE DATABASE piwordpress;
```

4. After this, create a username `wordpress` with the `password` password and give the user all privileges to the `piwordpress` database by entering this command:

```
> GRANT ALL PRIVILEGES ON piwordpress.* TO
"wordpress"@"localhost" IDENTIFIED BY "password";
```

5. Please replace `password` in the preceding code with something more secure. Then, reload the privileges and exit the MySQL shell with the following commands:

```
> FLUSH PRIVILEGES;
```

```
> EXIT
```

6. Next, give full write access to the `wordpress` directory for the setup process by running the following command:

```
# chmod a +w /srv/www/wordpress
```

7. Open the IP of the Raspberry Pi in the browser followed by `/wordpress/wp-admin/install.php`.

8. Go through the setup process using the parameters outlined in the fourth step. The tables prefix can be anything.

9. Finally, adjust the ownership and permissions by running the following commands:

```
# find /srv/www/wordpress -type d -exec chmod 755 {} \;
```

```
# find /srv//www/wordpress -type f -exec chmod 644 {} \;
```

```
# chown www-data:www-data /srv/www/wordpress/* -R
```

```
# chmod 400 /srv/www/wordpress/wp-config.php
```

The WordPress installation can now be accessed through `http://IP/wordpress` in your browser.

 WordPress and PHP have historically many security holes, and simple mistakes by a plugin or theme coder can make your Raspberry Pi vulnerable to attack. Take extra care by not storing sensitive information on the Raspberry Pi, installing a security plugin, configuring fail2ban, and monitoring your logs. Always search for more ways to secure your server and data.

Summary

In this chapter, an overview of the different operating systems was covered along with common administrative tasks. A full-featured web server with a personal website platform was set up.

In the next chapter, a media player will be added to the web server, allowing you to listen to your music from anywhere.

2
Developing Web Applications

Modern web technologies allow web pages to be used as full-featured applications to replace traditional programs. The most important of these is AJAX, which allows a page to communicate with the server and dynamically alter web page elements. In this chapter, you will learn the basics of web development by creating a simple web page, changing its visual appearance, and making it interactive. Then, you will learn how a web server can serve dynamic pages generated by Python, before putting all of these skills together to create a media player and radio station that you can access from anywhere. We will cover the following topics in this chapter:

- Adding page content with HTML
- Customizing the visual appearance
- Adding interactivity with JavaScript
- Simplifying scripts with jQuery
- An introduction to Python
- Creating an Internet radio station

Getting started with HTML, JavaScript, and jQuery

In the previous chapter, you were introduced to Raspberry Pi and installed LAMP server on your Raspberry Pi. You also installed WordPress to host your personal website/blogs. So, how do you create your blog/website? This section will give a high-level overview of HTML, CSS, JavaScript, and jQuery.

[If you are familiar with HTML, CSS, JavaScript, and jQuery, you might want to jump directly to the *An introduction to Python* section. You can get the source code from the book website.]

Adding page content with HTML

HTML is used by the web browser to display content. To get started, replace /srv/ www/index.php with the index.html file, which contains the following code:

```
<!DOCTYPE html>
<html lang="en">
<head>
  <meta charset="UTF-8">
  <title>Hello world</title>
</head>

<body>
  <h1>Hello World!</h1>
  <p>This is a <em>simple</em><abbr title=
  "HyperTextMarkup Language">HTML</abbr> example.</p>
  <!-- This is a comment -->
  <form class="exampleform">
    <p><input name="num1"> * <input name="num2"> =
    <span id="result"></span></p>
<button id="calculate">Calculate</button>
  </form>
</body>
</html>
```

Downloading the example code

You can download the example code files from your account at http://www.packtpub.com for all the Packt Publishing books you have purchased. If you purchased this book elsewhere, you can visit http://www.packtpub.com/support and register to have the files e-mailed directly to you.

Accessing the Raspberry Pi through the web browser should show how the preceding code is interpreted. The top line, <!DOCTYPE html>, specifies the document type, which in this case is HTML5. The rest of the document can be broken down into elements, tags, attributes, content and comments. This is well represented in the following diagram:

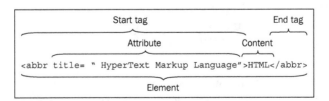

The components of an HTML element.

Tags are used to delimit elements. The start tags consist of angled brackets <...> containing the element's tag name, optionally followed by attributes. The end tags are similar, but the difference is that the opening bracket is followed by a / character and no attributes may be present. Void elements are those that are not allowed any content and do not require an end tag. In the preceding example, the void elements are meta and input. The tags must be nested. So, for example, `<b><i></i></b>` is valid, on the other hand, `<b><i></b></i>` is not.

Attributes are contained within the start tag and are of the form name = value. Where an attribute has a Boolean (true or false) value, it is sufficient to only include or exclude the attribute name to set it as true or false, respectively. Each element may have a set of attributes that have a specific meaning to that element. Global attributes are those that are applicable to all elements. In the preceding example, these are lang, id, and class. Where a value has spaces, quote marks must be used; otherwise, the spaces are optional. If quote marks are omitted and the attribute value contains spaces, each space will indicate the start of a new attribute.

The class and id attributes do nothing by themselves, but are useful for CSS and JavaScript. The class attribute can be applied to multiple elements on a page. The id, on the other hand, must be unique to a single element. For example, you can give class=border to multiple elements but you can't give id=point1 to multiple elements on a page.

Content is simply the content to which the tags apply. In the preceding code example, the content of the h1 element is Hello World!.

Finally, comments are text contained between the start delimiter <!-- and the end delimiter -->. These are not parsed by the browser and are only there for code readability.

The html element is the root of the HTML document and contains all other elements. The lang attribute is used to define the language of the element. Although optional, it is recommended as it helps spell checkers, speech synthesis programs as well as search engines.

The head element contains the document's metadata. The title element tells the browser and search engines what the document title is. This appears in the window and tab captions in the browser. The meta element has multiple purposes, but in the given example, it sets the character encoding declaration to Unicode. Again, this helps browsers and search engines to understand how to interpret the data.

The body element contains the non-metadata part of the HTML document.

The text formatting tags in the preceding example are h1, p, em, and abbr. These are used for headings, paragraphs, emphasis, and abbreviations, respectively. The 1 in h1 can be replaced with any number up to 6 for subheadings. When we apply the abbr element, the title attribute value is displayed when the mouse is over the element, and in our example, it will be the expansion of the abbreviation HTML.

As the name suggests, the form element is used for user-submittable forms. In the preceding example, this consists of two input elements and a button. The name attribute on the input elements is used to identify the data when it is submitted to the server or processed in a script. When the user clicks **Calculate**, the form data (num1 and num2) will be sent to the server using a GET request.

When a URL is entered, the browser sends a GET request. The server responds with a response header, which contains information to help the browser interpret the data. This is followed by a response body, which is the HTML document itself. When data is submitted with a GET request, it is appended to the URL. In the preceding example, ?num1=&num2= will be appended to the URL if the input fields were left blank.

The GET request works well for such cases, but there are situations where the POST request should be used instead. Data sent using this request may be arbitrarily large and is not stored by the browser once it's sent. However, neither methods offer any security and any data sent over HTTP is easily intercepted.

 The only way to post data securely is to use HTTPS, which is not covered in this book. Before making any site available online, consider the security implications to your server and your site visitors.

The remaining span element does not represent anything specific. It is a generic wrapper that will be used to store the answer.

As summaries written for beginners are usually incomplete, sometimes inaccurate and often misleading, whenever writing an HTML document, it is a good idea to have the relevant specification open. The HTML5 specification is accessible at http://www.w3.org/TR/html5/. If you are uncertain that the HTML document is valid, you can use W3C's validator to catch mistakes. The validator is accessible at http://validator.w3.org/.

Customizing the visual appearance

CSS is used to modify the appearance of HTML elements. In the same directory as index.html, you can create hello.css, which contains the following:

```
body {
  padding: 30px 30px;
```

```css
  font: 13px/100% Verdana, sans-serif;
  text-align: center;
}
body:after {
  content: "This text is generated using CSS";
  display: block;
  margin-top: 2em;
}
input {
  width: 50px;
}
span#result {
  width: 50px;
  display: inline-block;
}
form.exampleform {
  display: inline-block;
  border:1px solid;
  border-radius:20px;
  box-shadow: 5px 5px 2px #888888;
  padding: 20px;
}
```

Simply adding the file has no effect, so the following element must be added to the content of the head element of the index.html file:

```html
<link rel="stylesheet" href="hello.css" type="text/css">
```

The link element is used to define the relationship between documents. In this case, the attributes specify that the document should be linked to a stylesheet file hello.css of the type text/css.

Refreshing the page now should show the effect of the added stylesheet. To get a clear understanding of this, have a look at the following diagram:

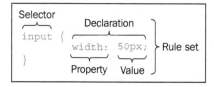

The components of a CSS rule set

 Different browsers (Chromium, Midori, and others) have different rendering engines. So sometimes, even if you are using the same CSS, your page/website will look different on different browsers.

The added CSS file contains five rule sets. Each rule set starts with a selector that is followed by a declaration block. The declaration block contains ; (semicolons), which are separated declarations in curly brackets {...}. Each declaration is made up of a property name followed by a : (colon) and a property value.

The selector is a pattern used to select which HTML elements the declaration block applies to. A summary of commonly used patterns is given here:

- *: All elements
- A: All A elements
- A B: All B elements descending from an A element
- A > B: All B elements that are children of an A element
- Please note the difference between descendants and children. Descendant elements can be nested in many levels deep, while children are elements nested directly within the parent element.
- A[att=test]: The A element containing attribute att matching test
- A.test: Elements A whose class attribute contains test
- A#test: Elements A whose id attribute matches test

:before and :after are pseudo-elements, which are used to prepend and append content to the element using the content property. These can be used to add bullet points and numbers to lists or quote marks for quoted text.

HTML elements inherit the CSS properties of their parent elements. For example, a heading containing a bold word will look different from a bold word in a paragraph. Whenever a property does get changed, it can be given the inherit value in order to force inheritance.

The comments within CSS documents begin with /* and end with */.

In the case that a property value is a length, it can be specified as a length relative to the font-size property, an absolute length or a percentage. In order to specify the nature of the length as a number, it should be directly followed by a unit identifier. The relative unit identifiers are em and ex, referring to the font point size and x-height, respectively. The absolute unit identifiers are in, cm, mm, pt, pc and px, which are used for inches, centimeters, millimeters, points, picas, and pixels respectively. Percentages use the % unit identifier, where the percentage is relative to the property value of the parent element.

Each visible element has a box that helps to define its positioning. The content of the element is surrounded by padding, a border and a margin, as shown here:

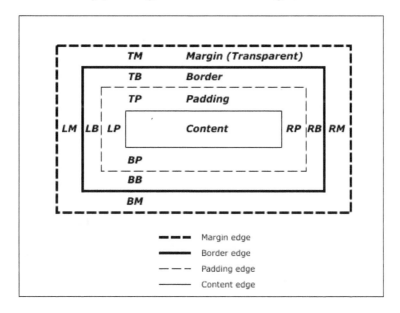

The CSS box mode showing how the margin, border, and padding properties affect the appearance. You can access this at `http://www.w3.org/TR/html5/`.

The padding area can be defined using the individual `padding-top`, `padding-right`, `padding-bottom`, and `padding-left` properties or a single `padding` property. Each element may be a fixed width or a percentage. The `padding` property can take multiple values. If a single value is given, it applies to all sides. The two values set the top and bottom sides. In the case of three values that are given, the first and third values set the top and bottom sides, while the second value sets the left and right sides. Giving all four value sets the top, right, bottom, and left sides to each individual value. The margins work the same way, using the `margin-top`, `margin-right`, `margin-bottom`, `margin-left`, and `margin` properties. The `border-width` property can be set using the same pattern. In the case that a border is the same on all sides, a single `border` property can be set by specifying any combination of width, color, and style (for example, solid, dashed, dotted, and so on).

Colors are specified using one of CSS color keywords, which are aqua, black, blue, fuchsia, gray, green, lime, maroon, navy, olive, orange, purple, red, silver, teal, white, and yellow. Alternatively, this can be via RGB notation, where RGB values are given as hexadecimal `#rgb`, `#rrggbb` (`#FF00EE`) values or by `rgb(r, g, b)`, where each color value is a positive integer up to 255(0xFF hex). Additionally, margin values may be auto, which calculates the values based on context.

The layout is also specified using the display, width, height, position, top, right, bottom, and left properties. The four direction properties are used to set the box offset of the element. The values have different meanings depending on the display and position combinations. The common display values are inline, inline-block, and block. In general, the inline elements flow with the text whereas block elements start a new line and utilize maximum horizontal space. The inline-block elements are somewhere in between as they shrink the size of their content and can flow with the page content. position is a complicated property, so for now, it is enough to know that the valid values are static, relative, absolute, and fixed.

As with HTML, to understand all of the intricate details of CSS, you should refer to the specification found at http://www.w3.org/TR/CSS2/. The CSS validator can be accessed via http://jigsaw.w3.org/css-validator/.

Adding interactivity with JavaScript

JavaScript is used to add interactivity to web pages. In the following example, the form is displayed but the calculation does not take place. You can do this by creating a hello.js file with the following content:

```
varcalc = document.getElementById('calculate');
var result = document.getElementById('result');
calc.onclick = function () {
  var num1 = calc.form.num1.value;
  var num2 = calc.form.num2.value;
  result.textContent = num1 * num2;
  return false;
}
```

In order to use the script, the following element must be within the body of the index.html document, as you can see here:

```
<script type=text/javascript src="hello.js"></script>
```

Alternatively, the entire script can be contained directly in the body of the HTML document within the <script>...</script> tags. Whenever a script does not interact directly with any elements on the page, it may be placed in the head element. In general, it is recommended to put all scripts just before the body end tag, as this allows the web page to load all page content first, ensuring the site feels responsive.

The `var` keyword is used to declare variables. In the preceding example, two global variables and two local variables are declared. Global variables are declared outside of all functions and are accessible by all functions. These may also be declared within functions by omitting the `var` keyword, although this method is not recommended. Local variables are only accessible within the scope they are declared. Referring to the previous example, the variables `num1` and `num2` exist only within the function block assigned to `calc.onclick`.

The `document` object provides a way to get information about the page. The `document` object's `getElementById` function takes the element ID as an argument and returns a reference to the element. As a result, the `calc` variable refers to the **Calculate** button and the `result` variable refers to the `span` element.

Functions can be defined using the following syntax:

```
function add (number1, number2){
    return number1 + number 2;
}
```

The `add()` function takes two arguments: `number1` and `number2`. This then returns the sum. For example, calling `add (5, 2);` will return `7`.

Alternatively, the same can be accomplished using the following code:

```
var add = function (number1, number2){
    return number1 + number2;
};
```

In this case, an `add` function is created and assigned to the `add` variable. Again, the function can be called as before, as variables can be functions.

Assigning a function to the button's `onclick` handler ensures that the function runs every time the button is clicked. The function reads the values of the input fields and assigns the product of the two as the content of the `span` element. `calc.form.num1.value` can be understood as "the value of field named `num1` in the form that `calc` belongs to". The function returns false, as a true value would submit the form and refresh the page, which is not desired in this case.

For more resources, you can visit `http://developer.mozilla.org/docs/Web/JavaScript`.

Simplifying scripts with jQuery

jQuery simplifies scripting by providing a quicker way to reference and modify elements, handle events, and communicate with the server without refreshing the page. In order to use jQuery, it must first be included in the HTML document. One method to do this is shown here:

1. First, download the compressed `.js` file from `http://jquery.com`.

2. Next, place it in the web page's directory

3. Finally, include it in the HTML document using `<script type=text/javascriptsrc="jquery-1.11.0.js"></script>`, as shown earlier.

However, there are advantages to letting Google's content distribution network (known as CDN) host jQuery for you. This can be done simply by setting the `src` attribute to `//ajax.googleapis.com/ajax/libs/jquery/1.11.0/jquery.min.js`. As other websites do this as well, chances are that many visitors will already have the file cached by their browser. This also reduces the load on your server and speed up loading times, as Google distributes its traffic across many servers.

 The use of `//` (leading double slashes) is used to ensure that the URL is of the same protocol that is currently in use. For example, whether you use HTTP or HTTPS, the jQuery file will be served over the same protocol.

Returning to hello.js, the code can be replaced with the following:

```
$(document).ready(function() {
  $("#calculate").click(function() {
   var num1 = $("input[name=num1"]).val();
    var num2 = $("input[name=num2"]).val();
    $"#result").text(num1 * num2);
    return false;
  });
});
```

jQuery's element selection method is similar to that of CSS, where you can include the selection pattern inside `$("...")`. The preceding example has five selectors using this pattern:

- `$(document)`: The document object represents the root of the HTML page

- `$("#calculate")`: This is an element with the `id` attribute set to `calculate`

- `$("#result")`: This is an element with the `id` attribute set to `result`

- `$("input[name=num1]")`: This is an element with the `name` attribute set to num1

- `$("input[name=num2]")`: This is an element with the `name` attribute set to num2.

JavaScript cannot work with elements that have not already loaded. `.ready` can be used to provide a handler function that executes when the element is ready for use. In the preceding example, an anonymous function is passed as the parameter to `$(document).ready`, which is executed once the HTML document has fully loaded.

Although it looks like there is more, the function passed to `$(document).ready` is a single statement. This is simply passing another anonymous function as the argument of `$("#calculate").click`. This binds the function to the **Calculate** button's click event.

Finally, the bound function multiplies the values of the input fields and passes the result to `$("#result").text`, which sets the span element's text to the given value. Again, a false value is returned to ensure the form has not submitted.

You can find complete documentation for jQuery at `http://api.jquery.com/`.

An introduction to Python

So far, only the client side of a web application or website has been covered. However, the bulk of the work is usually done on the server, rather than in the browser. Python is an excellent language to handle the backend of web applications and it is very well supported on Raspberry Pi. Moreover, it is the official programming language suggested by Raspberry Pi Foundation. Apart from web development, Python can also be used to develop desktop and command-line applications or games and to the interface of the Raspberry Pi to the real world. This makes it easy to create a web application to display sensor data, or to control the Raspberry Pi.

Python code can be tested directly by running the python command to enter the Python shell. Within the shell, statements can be entered directly. In order to exit the shell, enter `quit()` or press *Ctrl* + *D*. To run the code as a proper program, enter it into a file with the `.py` extension. The program can then be executed by running `python example.py`. However, this is still not ideal.

A **shebang**, which is the following combination #!, can be added to the start of a file to indicate which program should parse the file. For example, a file starting with #!/usr/bin/python will always be executed using Python. In order to make the file executable, you should run chmod +x example.py. The file can then be launched by simply running ./example.py as any other executable file.

 The current version of Python is 2.7, although 3.2 is becoming increasingly popular. Unfortunately, there are some minor syntax differences between the two, which means that some code written for Python 3.x will not run in Python 2.7. This mostly affects print statements without parenthesis.

An excellent resource to learn Python can be found at http://learnpythonthehardway.org/. The official documentation can be accessed through http://docs.python.org/2.7/.

Syntax

In JavaScript, curly braces were used to group statements, while indentation was added only for readability. Python, on the other hand, relies on indentation to group statements. Most commonly, tabs or multiples of four spaces are used for different indentation levels. Another major difference is the use of semicolons before the start of an indented block. This is demonstrated in the following snippet of code:

```
if (True):
    print ("foo")
```

Data types

The fundamental data types are numbers, strings, lists, tuples, and dictionaries. Each of these can be assigned as follows:

```
a = 3.14
b = "foo"
c = ("Mon", "Tue", "Wed", "Thu", "Fri", "Sat", "Sun")
d = ["Bread","Milk","Eggs","Tomatoes"]
e = {"James Stewart":2025550193, "Patricia Rayborn":2025550118}
```

Note that Python does not require a keyword to identify the variable type or to signify variable declaration. A variable set to a certain data type can be assigned a value of another data type later on.

The variable a is assigned the number 3.14. In order to convert an object to a string, the str function can be used. For example, a = str(a) would convert the variable a from a number to a string.

In order to assign a string to a variable, either single or double quote marks can be used. Strings can be concatenated (combined) using the + operand. If the string itself requires a quote mark, the escape character \ can be used. For example, "The value of b is \"" + b + "\"" will translate to **The value of b is "foo"**. Apart from using the escape character for quote marks, it may be used to start a new line (\n), add a tab (\t), or any other character. Since a string is an array of characters, individual characters of string can be indexed with square brackets. A range can be specified with the start and end character indices separated by a colon. For example, b[0] and b[1:2] will return **f** and **oo**, respectively.

The variable c is assigned a tuple value. Tuples are immutable lists, that is, they cannot have their values modified. The tuple elements may consist of any combination of data types, including other tuples. Similar to strings and other arrays, each element can be indexed as before.

Standard lists are similar to tuples, but the elements can be sorted, inserted, or removed. The following code will sort the list d, remove the element Eggs and insert it back to its original position:

```
d.sort ()
d.remove ('Eggs')
d.insert (2, 'Eggs')
```

Tuples are faster than lists and should be used where the elements can remain static. As shown in the preceding example, a constant sequence, such as the days in a week, are better suited to a tuple. However, a shopping list would need to be modified, so a list is preferred.

Finally, dictionaries are similar to lists, but are accessed by a key rather than an index number. For example, e['James Stewart'] will return **202555019**, but e[0] will return an error. In order to check if an element exists in the dictionary, the in keyword can be used, as shown here:

```
'foo' in e
False
'Patricia Rayborn' in e
True
```

Finally, the tuple, list, and dictionary values can be functions. Dictionaries are particularly useful here as they allow the value of a variable to determine which function to execute.

Decorators

Decorators allow functions to be extended and are used as follows:

```
def foo (func):
   print ("foo")
   return func
@foo
def bar ():
   print ("bar")
bar()
```

The function `foo` takes another function as an argument, prints **foo**, and then returns the given function. The `bar` function simply prints **bar**, but the `foo` decorator is added with the @ keyword. Whenever `bar` is called, it is passed as the parameter to `foo`. As a result, calling `bar` prints both **foo** and **bar**.

An example where this is useful could be as a range check to ensure that values passed to a function are valid where multiple functions require the same check. Without a range check decorator, each function would require the same snippet of code.

Modules

A set of functions can be saved to a file and then imported into another script. The filename, without the extension, is used as the module name. Once a module has been imported, Python searches for it in the current directory, with the directories listed in the PYTHONPATH environment variable and a set of other directories that are dependent on the particular installation.

Modules are imported using the `import` keyword. For example, the `os` module provides functions to interface with the operating system. The following snippet of code will import the `os` module and display the current working directory:

```
import os
print (os.getcwd())
```

Alternatively, the `from` keyword can be used so that the module does not have to be specified once a function has been called:

```
from os import getcwd
print (getcwd())
```

Flask

Flask provides a convenient way to use Python for web development. To demonstrate the basics, it will be used to extend the calculator example by providing a backend if JavaScript is not available.

Before getting started with Flask, it must be installed with the following command:

```
# apt-get install python-flask
```

Next, create a directory to store the Flask application and then two subdirectories named static and templates as shown:

```
$ mkdir -p ~/hello/static
$ mkdir ~/hello/templates
```

You should then move the HTML file into the templates directory and the CSS and JavaScript files into the static folder.

In the new directory, create a hello.py file with the following content:

```python
#!/usr/bin/python

from flask import Flask, request, render_template

app = Flask(__name__)

@app.route('/')
def hello():
  try:
    num1_string = request.args.get('num1')
    num2_string = request.args.get('num2')
    number1 = (float(num1_string) if '.' in num1_string else
      int(num1_string))
    number2 = (float(num2_string) if '.' in num2_string else
      int(num2_string))
    result = number1 * number2
return render_template('hello.html',
      num1 = number1, num2 = number2, result = result)
  except:
return render_template('hello.html')

if __name__ == '__main__':
  app.debug = True
  app.run(host = '0.0.0.0')
```

You can then make the file executable by running `chmod +x hello.py`.

The file introduces a few new concepts, but most of it should be familiar. The shebang (`#!`) ensures that the file is interpreted using the Python binary. Following this, the necessary functions from the Flask module are imported.

`__name__` is a global variable within Python that contains the module name. When the script is executed directly, rather than from another script, the `__name__` value is `__main__`. Before using Flask, the application object needs to be created, which takes the `__name__` global variable as the argument.

The application object's route function is used as a decorator to register functions to a URL. For example, if the pi's IP is 192.168.1.101, then `@app.route('/')` binds the `hello` function to the address `http://192.168.1.101/`.

The next new concept is exception handling using the `try` and `except` statements. When they are encountered, Python tries to execute the `try` clause. If no exceptions occur, the `except` clause is skipped. Otherwise, the rest of the `try` clause is skipped and the `except` clause is executed instead.

The `request.args.get()` function is used to receive the arguments passed by the GET request. Unfortunately, it returns a string, rather than a float or integer and Python cannot multiply strings. Since the entered number could be an integer or a float, the `int` or `float` function is used to convert the string depending on whether a decimal point is present in the string. If the GET request does not contain the `num1` and `num2` parameters, trying to make the conversion will throw an exception.

The line `number1 = (float(num1_string) if '.' in num1_string else int(num1_string))` can be rewritten as follows:

```
if '.' in num1_string:
    number1 = float(num1_string)
else:
    number1 = int(num1_string)
```

After both numbers have been converted, multiplied, and assigned to the `result` variable, the page itself is returned. The `render_template` function takes a filename as an argument along with optional variables, finds the file in the templates directory, and returns the page after processing it. If an error occurs while processing the number inputs, the page is rendered without passing any parameters.

Flask comes with a simple web server that is useful for development. If the file is run as a script directly, the server is launched using the application object's `run` function. Passing `host='0.0.0.0'` as the argument ensures that the server accepts connections from external IP addresses. Setting `app.debug` to `True` will display debug information about any errors that occur on the page. These features should not be used on a production server and are only useful for development. A typical server will load the Flask application as a module rather than run it directly, so the lines are inside an `if __name__ == '__main__'` clause. This ensures that when the application is deployed, it works and is less vulnerable to attack.

Before the application is properly functional, the HTML template file needs to be modified.

The static files are now no longer found where they were. By default, they are within the `static` folder. However, Flask can be configured in many different ways. For example, `hello.css` is now found in `static/hello.css`, but it could be in any arbitrary folder. To handle this, the `url_for` function is used. It is generally used to return the URL for a function. For example, `url_for('index')` would return `/`. However, when `static` is used as the function, it can be used to return the URL for a file when the `filename` parameter is passed.

The double curly brackets are used to ensure the content is not considered as typical HTML. You should modify the line that links in `hello.css` as follows:

```
<link rel="stylesheet" href="{{ url_for('static',
filename='hello.css') }}" type="text/css">
```

Next, make sure that the num1 and num2 variables passed by the `hello` function to `render_template` are displayed in the input boxes:

```
<p><input name="num1" type="number" value="{{ num1 }}"> * <input
name="num2" type="number" value="{{ num2 }}"> =
```

Finally, you can display the result:

```
<span id="result">{{ result }}</span></p>
```

In order to launch the application, run `./hello.py`. Note that the default port for the test server is 5000, so in order to access the application, enter the IP of Raspberry Pi, followed by `:5000`. Disabling JavaScript in your browser will show the fallback method working.

For further information about Flask, you can consult the official documentation at `http://flask.pocoo.org/docs/`.

Creating an Internet radio station

Although the previous example had no practical applications, it introduced most of the concepts needed to make something useful. To put the skills together in a more interesting way, the next example will show you how to create your own Internet radio station. A screenshot of the **piMusic** interface is shown here:

The piMusic interface

The aim is to develop a site to play music stored on your Raspberry Pi from anywhere. This will integrate a small file browser that will allow you to browse your music collection and click a file to play it. Clicking **Home** will return to the top of the music folder, whereas **Up** will go up one directory level. Instead of playing individual files, clicking **Radio** will allow you to play a radio station, which you can manage from your Raspberry Pi.

First, create and enter a directory for the new Flask application as follows:

```
$ mkdir -p ~/piMusic/static/music
$ mkdir ~/piMusic/templates
$ cd ~/piMusic/templates
```

Creating the user interface

There are two main ways to play audio from the browser. The first is using the HTML5 `audio` element. The downside is that very few browsers support MP3 playback. Although it is possible to keep multiple formats of all files and use JavaScript to determine which file should be played, this solution is tedious to implement. The second alternative is to use Flash to play the audio. jPlayer is a media player for jQuery that supports both of these methods. You can head over to `http://jplayer.org` to download jPlayer 2.5.0 and extract the `Jplayer.swf` and `jquery.jplayer.min.js` files into the `static` folder.

This download does not include a theme, so one needs to be obtained elsewhere. A web designer by the name of Luke McDonald has ported an audio player theme by premium-pixels for use with jPlayer and it can be downloaded from `http://github.com/lukemcdonald/jplayer-skins/archive/master.zip`. The `jplayer-skins/skins/premium-pixels` directory needs to be extracted into the `static` directory.

To get an interface that looks relatively clean and professional, Bootstrap is used. It provides templates for common web page elements in a CSS file as well as a JavaScript file for enhanced interactivity. If you wish, you may download it from `http://getbootstrap.com` or use the provided CDN.

To help visually separate files and directories in the file browser, they will be prepended with a relevant icon. `http://genericons.com` provides great-looking icons for free. Download and extract the archive into the `static` folder as before.

In the template directory, create `pimusic.html` with the following content:

```html
<!DOCTYPE html>
<html lang="en">
  <head>
    <meta charset="UTF-8">
    <title>piMusic</title>
    <link type="text/css" href="//netdna.bootstrapcdn.com/
bootstrap/3.1.1/css/bootstrap.min.css" rel="stylesheet"/>
    <link type="text/css" href="{{url_for('static', filename='premium-
pixels/premium-pixels.css') }}" rel="stylesheet"/>
    <link type="text/css" href="{{url_for('static',
filename='genericons/genericons.css') }}" rel="stylesheet"/>
  </head>
  <body>
    <script src="//ajax.googleapis.com/ajax/libs/jquery/1.11.0/jquery.
min.js"></script>
    <script type=text/javascript
    src="//netdna.bootstrapcdn.com/bootstrap
    /3.1.1/js/bootstrap.min.js"></script>
    <script type=text/javascriptsrc="{{ url_for('static',
    filename='jquery.jplayer.min.js') }}"></script>
  </body>
</html>
```

This template doesn't display much, but it includes the third-party tool that will be used. In order to add the navigation bar, you should insert the following code:

```html
<div class="navbar navbar-inverse navbar-fixed-top" role="navigation">
  <div class="container">
    <div class="navbar-header">
```

```
      <div class="navbar-brand">piMusic</div>
    </div>
    <ul class="nav navbar-nav">
      <li class="active"><a href="#" id='home'>Home</a></li>
      <li><a href="#" id='updir'>Up</a></li>
      <li><a href="#" id='radio'>Radio</a></li>
    </ul>
    <div class="nav navbar-nav navbar-right">

    </div>
  </div>
</div>
```

This code is based on the `navbar` template provided in the Bootstrap documentation. The top `div` has three classes, which identifies it as a navigation bar with inverted colors, fixed to the top of the page. The next `div` serves as a container for the rest of the elements, which centers the content and assigns the correct widths. After a Pi MusicBox brand is added, the actual menu items are added as an unordered list. The highlighted element is a right-aligned navigation element that will contain jPlayer. To add it, use the following code:

```
<div id="jquery_jplayer_1" class="jp-jplayer"></div>
<div id="jp_container_1" class="jp-audio">
  <div class="jp-type-single">
    <div class="jp-guijp-interface">
      <ul class="jp-controls">
        <li><a href="javascript:;" class="jp-previous"
        tabindex="1">previous</a></li>
        <li><a href="javascript:;" class="jp-play"
        tabindex="1">play</a></li>
        <li><a href="javascript:;" class="jp-pause"
        tabindex="1">pause</a></li>
        <li><a href="javascript:;" class="jp-next"
        tabindex="1">next</a></li>
        <li><a href="javascript:;" class="jp-stop"
        tabindex="1">stop</a></li>
        <li><a href="javascript:;" class="jp-mute" tabindex="1"
        title="mute">mute</a></li>
        <li><a href="javascript:;" class="jp-unmute" tabindex="1"
        title="unmute">unmute</a></li>
        <li><a href="javascript:;" class="jp-volume-max"
        tabindex="1" title="max volume">max volume</a></li>
      </ul>
      <div class="jp-progress">
        <div class="jp-seek-bar">
```

```
                    <div class="jp-play-bar"></div>
                </div>
            </div>
            <div class="jp-volume-bar">
                <div class="jp-volume-bar-value"></div>
            </div>
            <div class="jp-time-holder">
                <div class="jp-current-time"></div>
                <div class="jp-duration"></div>
            </div>
            <ul class="jp-toggles">
                <li><a href="javascript:;" class="jp-shuffle" tabindex="1"
                title="shuffle">shuffle</a></li>
                <li><a href="javascript:;" class="jp-shuffle-off"
                tabindex="1" title="shuffle off">shuffle off</a></li>
                <li><a href="javascript:;" class="jp-repeat" tabindex="1"
                title="repeat">repeat</a></li>
                <li><a href="javascript:;" class="jp-repeat-off"
                tabindex="1" title="repeat off">repeat off</a></li>
            </ul>
        </div>
        <div class="jp-no-solution">
            <span>Update Required</span>
            To play the media you will need to either update your
            browser to a recent version or update your <a
            href="http://get.adobe.com/flashplayer/"
            target="_blank">Flash plugin</a>.
        </div>
    </div>
</div>
```

This is a standard template provided by jPlayer, modified for the theme and to fit the navigation bar.

The last major element to add is the file browser itself, which is done by inserting the following code at the end of all the added div elements, before the script elements:

```
<div class="panel panel-default">
        <div class="panel-body">
            <ul id="files" class="filebrowser">
            </ul>
        </div>
    </div>
```

The first two `div` elements here are used by Bootstrap to create a panel, where an empty list will be stored. This list will be dynamically populated by a script, which will use the `files` ID to find the list. The `filebrowser` class will be used for theming.

To complete the frontend of the application, create a file named `pimusic.css` in the static directory with the following code:

```css
body {
    padding-top: 70px;
}
ul.filebrowser {
    list-style-type: none;
}
a.file:before {
    content: '\f452';
    font: normal 16px/1 'Genericons';
}
a.dir:before {
    content: '\f301';
    font: normal 16px/1 'Genericons';
}
.panel {
    width: 50%;
    margin-left: auto;
    margin-right: auto;
}
```

Then, include it in the HTML document by adding the following line to the head element:

```html
<link type="text/css" href="{{url_for('static',
filename='pimusic.css') }}" rel="stylesheet"/>
```

When the navigation bar is fixed to the top, it will overlap with the content of the page. The CSS file adds 70 pixels to the `body` element to avoid this problem.

Next, the bullets are removed from unordered lists of the `filebrowser` class. These are replaced with the `Genericons` icons by prepending links of `file` and `dir` classes with the relevant content. The content property for these icons is obtained from the *Genericons* website.

Finally, the panel is set to take up half of the screen's width and centered.

Writing the backend

Before adding interactivity to the site, there needs to be a clear way for JavaScript to interact with the server.

The backend will need to handle the following actions:

- Display the page
- Check whether the current directory is valid
- List the directories and MP3 files in the current directory
- Handle clicks on directories and files
- Go up a directory as well as return to the home directory

To begin, create the piMusic.py file in the main application directory with the following content:

```python
#! /usr/bin/python
from flask import Flask, render_template, session, \
    request, url_for, safe_join
from os import listdir, path
from json import dumps

app = Flask(__name__)
app.secret_key= \
'\x9bT\xcb\x87vp\x82u\xd1\x0ey\x8a\xfdtdW6\x12\xb1\xf16,\xa4\xb5'
startdir = app.static_folder + "/music/"
@app.route('/')
def index():
  return render_template('pimusic.html')

if __name__ == '__main__':
    app.debug=True
    app.run(host='0.0.0.0')
```

 The \ character is used to break long lines. In this case, it tells Python to treat the next line as a continuation of the previous. This approach is not recommended and is only used for presentation purposes.

Make it executable by running the chmod command as earlier:

```
$ chmod +x piMusic.py
```

Apart from the secret key, all of the content should look familiar. The application will use cookies to store the current directory so that multiple clients can browse the files without interfering. For security reasons, Flask encrypts session information using a secret key. In order to generate the secret key, open up a Python shell and execute the following commands:

```
import os
os.urandom(24)
```

Then, replace the highlighted section of the code with the output.

Next, the function to check whether the current directory is valid needs to be added:

```
def checkcurrdir():
if ('currdir' not in session or
no tsafe_join(session['currdir'],"").startswith(startdir) or
not path.isdir(session['currdir'])):
        session['currdir'] = startdir
```

The `if` statement contains three conditions to determine whether a directory is valid:

- `'currdir' not in session`: The session does not have the variable `currdir` set at all

- `not safe_join(session['currdir'],"").startswith(startdir)`: The current directory is outside the home directory

- `path.isdir(session['currdir'])`: The current directory is not actually a directory

If any of these conditions are met, the directory is set back to the home directory.

Next, a function to list the valid files in the current directory is needed:

```
def listloc(loc):
  filetypes = {}
  files = listdir(loc)
  files = [elem for elem in files if (not elem.startswith('.') and
    (elem.lower().endswith(".mp3")   or
    path.isdir(safe_join(session['currdir'], elem))))]
  for index in range(len(files)):
    htclass = ("file", "dir")[
      path.isdir(safe_join(loc, files[index]))]
    filetypes[files[index]] = htclass
  return dumps(filetypes, sort_keys=True)
```

This function is a little complicated. First, an empty dictionary called `filetypes` is created. This will contain all of the valid entries of a directory and the information on whether they are directories or files.

Then, the files variable is created and is assigned a list of everything in the directory passed to the function. This list needs to only include directories and MP3 files, without any hidden files or directories. The way this is done in Python is difficult to understand at first, so a few simple examples need to be covered, as you can see here:

```
>>> a = [0, 1, 2, 3]
>>> [elem for elem in a]
[0, 1, 2, 3]
>>> [elem * 2 for elem in a]
[0, 2, 4, 6]
>>>[elem for elem in a if elem > 1]
[ 2, 3]
```

In the first case, a list containing all the elements in the list a is returned. Next, instead of simply returning the elements as they are, they are multiplied by two. In the final example, elements are returned as they are, but only if they are greater than one.

This same technique is used to filter the files. The files list is mapped back to itself, but only the elements that satisfy all of the following conditions are returned:

1. `not elem.startswith('.')`: The file is not hidden.
2. `elem.lower().endswith(".mp3")`: The file is an MP3 file *or*
3. `path.isdir(safe_join(session['currdir'], elem))`: The file is a directory.

 Only files that meet the first condition and either the second or third conditions are retained.

Once the list is filtered, it can be used to populate the dictionary. To do this, the function loops through each element in the list using the `for` loop. `range(len(files))` returns a list of indices for the files list, so each iteration of the for loop, using `files[index]` will return the next file.

`htclass = ("file", "dir")[path.isdir(safe_join(loc, files[index]))]` is another tricky line to understand. `htclass` is set to either `file` or `dir`, depending on whether the current element in the file list is an actual file or a directory. This is done by indexing a tuple with a `true` or `false` value. If the index is `false`, the first element is returned, but if it's `true`, the second value is returned.

The `filetypes` dictionary is populated using `filetypes[files[index]]=htcl`
`ass`. However, the purpose is to return a list of files and assign them to a relevant
class using JavaScript, and to do so, the dictionary needs to be converted to a format
JavaScript understands. One such format is called JSON. Python's `json` module
contains the `dumps` function, which can convert Python data into the JSON format.
The `return dumps(filetypes, sort_keys=True)` statement returns the dictionary
in the JSON format sorted by filenames.

A directory click can be handled with the following function:

```
def dirclick(req):
    if 'id' not in req.form:
return listloc(session['currdir'])
    clickeddir = path.normpath(safe_join(session['currdir'],
      req.form['id']))
if path.isdir(clickeddir):
        session['currdir'] = clickeddir
    checkcurrdir()
return listloc(session['currdir'])
```

The function will be passed through the POST request containing the clicked
directory name in the `id` variable. If the request does not contain the `id` variable,
it will simply return the list of files in the current directory.

Otherwise, the clicked directory path is normalized. Normalizing a path means
converting a path that looks like /home/pi/../pi into /home/pi. Although both
are valid, if the path is not normalized, a POST request can be crafted in a way that
will allow a hacker to list all the files on your Raspberry Pi.

The function then checks whether the clicked directory is a real directory, sets the
`currdir` variable in the session to the clicked directory, checks whether it is still
valid, and returns a list of files in the newly entered directory.

File clicks can be handled in a similar way:

```
def fileclick(req):
    if 'id' not in req.form:
return listloc(session['currdir'])
    clickedfile = safe_join(session['currdir'], req.form['id'])
if path.isfile(clickedfile):
        clickedfile = url_for('static',
        filename = clickedfile.replace(app.static_folder+'/',''))
return clickedfile
    return 0
```

The difference is that instead of listing files in a directory, the URL for the clicked file is returned, after making sure it is a valid file. The URL is generated by stripping the static folder location from the absolute path and using the url_for function. For example, if the path is /home/pi/piMusic/static/music/file1.mp3, stripping the static folder will return music/file1.mp3 and url_for will ensure the URL for the file is valid by returning /static/music/file1.mp3.

> Flask allows you to use a custom static folder or return URLs without the static directory specified. The code is written in a way that allows flexibility if you decide to change the default behavior, so some checks and conversions may seem redundant, but they serve a purpose.

The next function implements going up a directory:

```
def updir(req):
    session['currdir'] = path.split(session['currdir'])[0]
    checkcurrdir()
return listloc(session['currdir'])
```

The path.split statement is used to split the current directory into the path containing the directory and the directory itself. The first of these is then indexed and set as the current directory. The directory is then checked and listed.

The last function is to return to the home directory:

```
def rethome(req):
    session['currdir'] = startdir
return listloc(session['currdir'])
```

This simply sets the current directory to the home directory and returns its listing.

Finally, there needs to be a way to expose these functions fully for use with JavaScript:

```
@app.route('/_action', methods=['POST'])
def action():
    checkcurrdir()
    return { 'dirclick' : dirclick,
        'fileclick' : fileclick,
        'updir' : updir,
        'home' : rethome
    }[request.form['action']](request)
```

This function checks the current directory then calls one of the defined functions with the request object and the parameter. Which function is called is then determined by the `action` variable passed in the POST request. This is implemented by a dictionary where each action corresponds to a function. The dictionary is indexed by the relevant `action` and the request is passed as the parameter.

Connecting the user interface to the backend

Now that the backend and user interface is laid out, the last thing to do is connect the two using JavaScript.

One problem with using a separate JavaScript file is that it cannot use features provided by Flask's template features. For example, `url_for` will not work. Therefore, all content that requires such features should be included directly in the HTML template. In this case, the path for jPlayer's Flash file and the URL for the `action` function are needed.

Open the HTML template `pimusic.html` and insert the following script element before the other scripts:

```
<script type=text/javascript>
   var STATIC_LOC = "{{ url_for('static', filename='') }}";
   var ACTION_LOC = "{{ url_for('action') }}";
</script>
```

This will allow the `STATIC_LOC` and `ACTION_LOC` variables to be used in external scripts.

Next, create a file named `pimusic.js` in the `static` directory and add the following line at the end of the other script elements:

```
<script type=text/javascript src="{{ url_for('static',
filename='pimusic.js') }}"></script>
```

Open the newly created JavaScript file and add the following function:

```
function showdata(data) {
  var items = [];
  $.each(data, function (key, val) {
    items.push('<li><a href="#" id ="' + key + '" class ="' + val
    + '">' + key + "</a></li>");
  });
  $("#files").html(items);
}
```

The function steps through each data element using jQuery's iterator each the syntax for which is .each(collection, callback(indexInArray, valueOfElement)). The argument is the listing of the current directory along with the type of each element (file or dir). The items array is used to store list items that will be added to the file browser. The key, which is the filename, is used as the ID attribute value and content, while the value, which is the element type, is used as the class. Once the array is populated, its content is set as the content of the list identified by the ID of files using the following line: $("#files").html(items);.

Next, add a function to play a file:

```
function playfile(file) {
  $("#jquery_jplayer_1").jPlayer("setMedia", {
    mp3: file
  });
  $("#jquery_jplayer_1").jPlayer("play", 0);
}
```

The function takes the URL of an MP3 file or stream as a parameter, sets it as the current media for jPlayer and then plays it.

Next, the functions need to be bound to the relevant elements:

```
$("ul#files").on("click", "a.dir", function () {
$.post(ACTION_LOC, {
  action: "dirclick",
  id: this.id
  },
  showdata,
  "json");
});
```

This binds a function to the list of files and propagates to all elements identified by dirid. The fact that this function binds to the list rather than the a.dir elements is important. When this snippet of code is parsed by the browser, there are no a.dir elements and they change every time the directory is changed. Therefore, the function must be bound to an existing element and use a selector to specify which elements the function will actually apply to when the click is detected.

The function itself sends a post request to the ACTION_LOC URL, containing the action name, which is dirclick and the ID of the clicked directory, which corresponds to its name.

The same approach applies to file clicks:

```
$("ul#files").on("click", "a.file", function () {
$.post(ACTION_LOC, {
  action: "fileclick",
  id: this.id
  },
  playfile,
  "text");
});
```

However, instead of displaying a directory listing, the file is played. Next step is to bound the **Up** link:

```
$("a#updir").on("click", function () {
$.post(ACTION_LOC, {
  action: "updir",
  },
  showdata,
  "json");
});
```

As the **Up** link is not dynamically created, it is bound without specifying a selector as was done before. Next step is to bound the **Home** click event:

```
$("a#home").on("click", function () {
$.post(ACTION_LOC, {
  action: "home",
  },
  showdata,
  "json");
});
```

The **Home** click is a straightforward POST request with the home action and a `showdata` callback. Next step is to play an corresponding HTTP MP3-encoded file based on click event:

```
$("a#radio").on("click", function () {
  playfile('http://' + location.hostname + ':8000');
});
```

The preceding function will play an HTTP MP3-encoded audio stream running on the server's port 8000. **Music Player Daemon (MPD)** will be used to provide the stream.

Next, set jPlayer's Flash file location and tell it to use Flash if available, but fallback to HTML otherwise:

```
$("#jquery_jplayer_1").jPlayer({
swfPath: STATIC_LOC,
solution: "flash, html"
});
```

You can swap `html` and `flash` if you would like to try the HTML solution first and fall back to Flash.

```
$.post(ACTION_LOC, {
    action: "dirclick"
},
showdata,
"json");
```

As you can see from the preceding code, the final POST request is used to fill the file browser's list by sending a `dirclick` action with no ID.

At this stage, the application is complete. You may wish to extend it by adding support to upload files, playlists, creating your own themes, or turning it into a full-featured media library and player.

Setting up MPD

The final step is to run an actual Internet radio stream on Raspberry Pi. In order to do this, install MPD and the command-line client to control it by running the following command:

```
# apt-get install mpdmcp
```

Next, edit the configuration file found in `/etc/mpd.conf` according to the documentation in the file. For this application, the `music_directory` parameter was changed to the application's `music` folder location, and `db_file` was changed to the same location with the filename `tag_cache`. The `auto_update` statement is set to `yes` and the following output was added:

```
audio_output {
        type            "httpd"
        name            "piMusic"
        encoder         "lame"
        port            "8000"
        bitrate         "128"
        format          "44100:16:1"
}
```

Once MPD is configured, enter the following command to restart it:

```
# service mpd restart
```

The `mpc` command can then be used to control MPD. Familiarize yourself with the available commands by running `man mpc`. As an example, the following should get all of the files playing in random order:

```
mpc install | mpc add
mpc play
mpc random
mpc repeat
```

Now, clicking the radio button in the Flask application should tune into the MPD stream.

Deploying Flask applications

As mentioned earlier, running Flask applications by directly launching the script works for testing, but is extremely unsafe and slow. In order to use nginx as the server for Pi MusicBox, the following needs to be added to the server block of the nginx site's configuration file (`/etc/nginx/sites-available/pisite`):

```
location = /piMusic { rewrite ^ /piMusic/; }
location /piMusic { try_files $uri @piMusic; }
location @piMusic {
include uwsgi_params;
    uwsgi_param SCRIPT_NAME /piMusic;
    uwsgi_modifier1 30;
    uwsgi_passunix:/tmp/uwsgi.sock;
}
```

For consistency, the Pi MusicBox directory should be moved to `/srv`.

Next, uWSGI needs to be installed and configured. You can think of it as the glue that will connect your application to nginx. You can install it by running this:

```
# apt-get install uwsgi uwsgi-plugin-python
```

Then, create the app configuration file `/etc/uwsgi/apps-available/piMusic.ini` as follows:

```
[uwsgi]
plugins = python
socket =  /tmp/uwsgi.sock
```

```
module = piMusic
callable = app
processes = 4
master = 1
pythonpath = /srv/piMusic
```

Following this, link it into the apps-enabled directory, as shown here:

```
# ln -s /etc/uwsgi/apps-available/piMusic.ini /etc/nginx/sites-enabled/
```

Change the owner and permissions of the Pi MusicBox directory files to ensure that the web server can access the files but other users cannot:

```
# chown www-data:www-data /srv/piMusic -R
```

```
# chown mpd:audio /srv/piMusic/static/music/tag_cache
```

```
# find /srv/piMusic/ -type d -exec chmod 755 {} -R \;
```

```
# find /srv/piMusic/ -type f -exec chmod 644 {} -R \;
```

The first command changes the owner of all the files to the user and group www-data. The second line sets the MPD library file's ownership back to the user mpd and group audio. The third line makes all of the directories writeable by the owner, but readable and listable by everybody. The final lines not only make all the files readable by everyone, but also writeable by the owner.

This particular set of permissions serves as an example only. Although they work for the application, making the files writeable by the web server when they don't have to be is a potential security problem.

Summary

In this chapter, an important set of technologies for web development was covered and an application that takes advantage of them was developed. The skills gained here can be used to create rich web applications to control Raspberry Pi and attach hardware remotely.

In the next chapter, you will get introduced to Raspberry Pi electronics and some of the electronics components that you will use later in this book. Using this knowledge, you will develop a digital clock, an e-mail notifier, and an alarm clock.

3
Introduction to Electronics

As previously stated many times in this book, the true value of Raspberry Pi comes from its flexibility. This stands true for the electronics, where the **General Purpose input/output** (**GPIO**) pins allow Raspberry Pi to connect to different sensors and electronic components. In plain English, this means that the GPIO pins connect Raspberry Pi to the real world.

In this chapter, you will learn the basic laws of electronics, which is of absolute importance for creating electronics projects with your Raspberry Pi. Along with this, you will be introduced to various electronics components that will be used in the later part of this chapter to make an e-mail notifier and alarm clock. In this chapter, we will cover the following topics:

- Basic laws of electronics
- Introduction to different electronic components
- Introduction to Raspberry Pi electronics
- Developing a digital clock
- Developing an e-mail notifier
- Developing an alarm clock

Understanding the physics behind electronics

Electronics is the study of how electrons flow across different materials or space when subject to a variety of conditions.

To remind you of what an electron is, they exist as a negatively charged "cloud" of particles that orbit the nucleus, this itself consisting of protons (positively charged) and neutrons (electrically neutral). The atom is then made up of both the nucleus and the orbiting electrons.

These various materials can be classified into three categories based on their conductivity, which means the degree to which a specified material conducts or transfers electricity:

- **Conductors** have a large number of free electrons that can flow freely in the materials in one or the other direction. As a result, they have the highest conductivity amongst all three types. Some examples of conductors are copper and aluminum. Most of the electrical cables that you see are made of copper because they can carry electricity along its length without much loss.

- **Nonconductors** or insulators are the materials whose internal electrons do not flow freely because of the arrangement of the electrons and protons inside the material structure. Some examples are glass, paper, Teflon, rubber-like polymer, and most plastics. Such materials are used for insulating electrical cables for safety purposes as well as to avoid unnecessary loss. Please note that a perfect conductor or a perfect insulator does not exist in reality, and can only be used for the purposes of modeling (an ideal conductor or insulator).

- **Semiconductor** materials have conductivity that lies between a conductor and insulator but which is mainly dependent on the temperature, on a macroscopic level. The important point to note is that as the temperature increases, the conductivity of the semiconductor increases. This is different in the case of the conductor, where the conductivity will decrease due to the increase in resistance (covered in the next section).

Please note that a detailed discussion on this is outside the scope of this book. I would recommend that you find a physics university or college-level textbook for further study.

Semiconductors are the foundation of the modern electronics, including transistors, analog and digital integrated circuits, and **light-emitting diodes** (LED). Transistors, LEDs, and other modern electronics components will be introduced in a later part of this chapter.

Charge, voltage, current, and resistance

Charge, voltage, and current are the three important terms that you should know. Like mass, charge is a fundamental property or label for an atom, but no one really knows what this is. As a label, charge can be represented and measured in the real world. Just like gravity is the name of the force between masses that can be felt and measured, the electrostatic force was observed by scientists (and all manner of people); that bodies under certain electrical conditions also exerted forces on each another. As this can also be measured, a label called charge was invented to explain the observation, in the same way that mass was used to explain gravity.

Charge can be positive or negative, where the electron has a negative charge while the proton has a positive charge. This is measured in units of Coulombs, abbreviated as C, with the unit named to honor Charles Augustin Coulomb (1736-1806). He was the French aristocrat and engineer who first measured the force between charged objects using a sensitive torsion balance he invented. The important point to remember is that opposite charges attract each other while similar charges repel, meaning it requires some force to keep two opposite charges separated or two similar charges together. This is similar to gravity in the sense that it requires some force to keep an apple falling on the ground and to raise a big mass against gravity.

The potential that separates two points/charges is called voltage. In technical terms, voltage is the electrical potential difference between two points. It is measured in units of volts, abbreviated as V. The unit was named to honor Volta, an Italian scientist.

A flow of electric charge is called a current. The current flows in the direction from a higher voltage to lower voltage.

> The conventional current represents the flow from positive to negative; following the direction that independent, positively charged particles would travel. Nonconventional current represents the flow in the opposite direction (from negative to positive) and is the direction in which electrons would flow.

There is the potential for some confusion here because electrons (the charge carriers in a circuit) flow from a lower voltage to higher voltage. So, the direction of the current is represented as opposite to the flow of electrons.

Current is measured in amperes (*a*), amps for short, and was named after André-Marie Ampère, another French scientist who worked mostly with magnetic effects. An ampere is defined as a flow of one Coulomb of charge in one second after some point.

Electrical current is of two types: **direct current (DC)** and **alternating current (AC)**. In DC, the direction of charge does not change, so in other words, this is unidirectional flow of charge. In AC however, the movement of charges periodically reverses direction.

 All of the home appliances and electronic hardware, including Raspberry Pi, run on DC supply. The conventional symbols for representing charge, voltage, and current are Q, V, and I respectively.

Another important term that you should know is resistance. It is the inverse quantity of conductance, so in simple terms, resistance is the degree to which a specified material resists electricity.

 You can think of this like friction as it is something that resists the relative motion of two surfaces. Similarly, resistance is something that resists the flow of electrons in the material.

The conventional symbol for resistance is R. To honor the German physicist, Georg Ohm, it is measured in Ohms.

Basic laws of electronics

The most basic law of electronics are Ohm's law and Kirchhoff's law.

Ohm's law

Ohm's law deals with the relationship between voltage and current in an ideal conductor. This relationship states that:

The potential difference (voltage) across an ideal conductor is proportional to the current through it.

The constant of proportionality is called the resistance, R, which has already been described in the previous section. Ohm's law is given as follows:

V = I R

Here, I is the current through the conductor in units of amperes, V is the potential difference measured across the conductor in units of volts, and R is the resistance of the conductor in units of ohms.

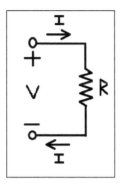

Kirchhoff's law

Kirchhoff's law is the starting point for analysis of any circuit. In 1845, Gustav Kirchhoff, a German physicist, first described two laws that became central to electrical engineering. The laws were generalized from the work of Georg Ohm. These two laws are:

1. **Kirchhoff's Current Law (KCL).**
2. **Kirchhoff's Voltage Law (KVL).**

Kirchhoff's Current Law (KCL)

KCL, also known as Kirchhoff's first law, Kirchhoff's point rule, or Kirchhoff's junction, rule states that:

The algebraic sum of currents in a network of conductors meeting at a point is zero.

Since current is the flow of electrons through a conductor, it cannot build up at a junction, meaning that current is conserved: what comes in must come out.

To simply put it, KCL is really conservation of charge. This can be stated as: *The algebraic sum of currents getting into a junction equals the sum of the currents getting out of the junction.*

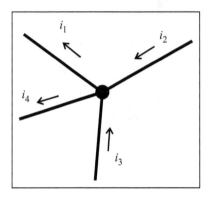

In the preceding circuit diagram, if we apply the KCL at the junction, then it will look like this:

$$i_2 + i_3 = i_1 + i_4$$

Kirchhoff's Voltage Law (KVL)

Kirchhof's Voltage Law, KVL, also known as Kirchhoff's second law, or Kirchhoff's loop (or mesh) rule, is defined as:

"The algebraic sum of the voltage (potential) differences in any loop must equal zero."

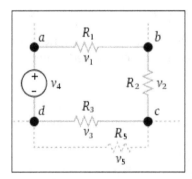

In the preceding circuit, if we apply the KVL, it will be as follows:

$$v_1 + v_2 + v_3 - v_4 = 0$$

This can also be written as:

$$v_1 + v_2 + v_3 = v_4$$

So, KVL can also be written as:

> *"The algebraic sum of the products of the resistances of the conductors and the currents in them in a closed loop is equal to the total power supply/voltage available in that loop."*

Electronics components

Having understood the basic laws of electronics, this section introduces you to the basic electronics components that are used in most of the electronics circuits.

Resistors

A resistor is a passive two-terminal electrical component that resists the flow of electrons as a circuit element. The current through a resistor is in direct proportion to the voltage across the resistor's terminals. This relationship is represented by an alternative representation of Ohm's law, which yields the current I as the ratio of the potential difference V to the resistance R:

I= V/R

The symbol used for a resistor in a circuit diagram varies from standard to standard and one country to another:

In the real world, a typical axial lead carbon resistor will look like this:

The value of the resistor can be measured by using the color code marked on them. The color bands of carbon resistors can be four, five, or six bands.

[In this book, four color band carbon resistors will be used.]

The first two bands represent the first two digits of resistance in ohms. The third band represents multiplier and the fourth band represents tolerance.

Values corresponding to a particular band can be found out using the following table:

Color	First Two Digits	Multiplier	Tolerance
Black	0	100	-
Brown	1	101	± 1%
Red	2	102	± 2%
Orange	3	103	-
Yellow	4	104	-
Green	5	105	-
Blue	6	106	-
Violet	7	107	-
Grey	8	108	-
White	9	109	-
Silver	-	10-2	± 10%
Gold	-	10-1	± 5%

For example, the value of a four band carbon resistor having color bands Red, Green, Red, and Silver will be:

25*100=2500 ohms with 10% tolerance

So, in general, the value of carbon resistor will be (AB*C) Ohms with D tolerance, where A = the value corresponding to first band by referring to the "First Two Digits" column in the preceding table. In preceding example, the Red band corresponds to the value 2.

 B = This is the value corresponding to the second band by referring to the "First Two Digits" column in the preceding table. In the preceding example, the Green band corresponds to 5.

C = This is the value corresponding to the third band by referring to the "Multiplier" column in the preceding table. In the preceding example, Red band corresponds to 100.

D= This is the value corresponding to the fourth band by referring to "Tolerance" columns in preceding table. In the preceding example, the Silver band corresponds to the value 10%.

In electrical circuits, it may happen that the exact value of resistor that is required might not be available, so sometimes, it is required to connect multiple resistors in series/parallel to get the required resistor value.

In a series configuration, the current through all of the resistors is the same, but the voltage across each resistor will be in proportion to its resistance. The potential difference (voltage) seen across the network is the sum of those voltages, thus the total resistance can be found as the sum of those resistances:

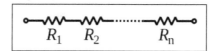

So, the equivalent resistor for the preceding case will be:

$$R_{eq}=R_1+R_2+...+R_n$$

Resistors in a parallel configuration are at the same potential difference (voltage); however, the currents through them get added at junction and can be of different value based on resistor value. The conductance (inverse of resistance) of the resistors then add to determine the conductance of the network:

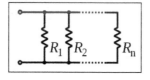

So, the equivalent resistor for the preceding case will be:

$$1/R_{eq} = 1/R_1 + 1/R_2 + ... + 1/R_n$$

Diodes

The resistor will block the flow of current in both directions. A diode is a two-terminal electronics component that has low resistance in one direction and high resistance in other direction. Diodes are mostly made up of silicon. The commonly used symbol for a diode is shown in the *common electronics components* table. LEDs are the most commonly used diodes in any electronics circuit. LED stands for Light Emitting Diode, so it emits light and sufficient voltage is provided across the LED anode and cathode. The longer lead of the LED is anode and the other end is cathode. The color of the light depends on the semiconductor material used in the LED, as shown in the following diagram:

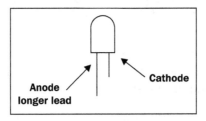

Switches

A switch is a component that interrupts the flow of current or diverts it from one conductor to another. There are few concepts such as debounce, interrupts, and polling that you need to know for better understanding of certain things. In mechanical switches, when the two contacts strikes, their momentum and elasticity act together to cause them to bounce apart one or more times before making a steady contact. In sensitive analog circuits, this will cause misinterpretation of the ON-OFF pulse and may lead to undesirable behavior of the circuits. To avoid this, debouncing circuits are used.

In order to understand debouncing circuits however, you first need to understand the concepts of interrupts and polling:

- **Polling** means constantly looking for something. This can be applied in software to any user interface where the microcontroller can poll the I/O pins to check whether there are any user inputs.

- On the other hand, **interrupts** use hardware to implement a more efficient way to know the controller that user inputs or a certain event has occurred. For example, your software scripts will constantly look for the certain I/O pin to check a user input is received or not, while on the other hand, when you insert the USB keyboard to Raspberry Pi, it will generate the interrupt and notify the firmware, which in turn stops the current processing task and load the keyboard driver (or actions related to that interrupt). Once this is completed, it will resume the last processing task. The following table has information about commonly used switches:

Switch name	Expansion of abbreviation	Description	Symbol
SPST	Single Pole Single Throw	This is a simple ON-OFF switch where two terminals are either connected or disconnected.	
SPDT	Single Pole Double Throw	This is a simple changeover switch. **COMz** (Common) can either be connected to **L1 or L2**.	
DPST	Double Pole Single Throw	This is equivalent to two SPST switches controlled by a single mechanism.	

Switch name	Expansion of abbreviation	Description	Symbol
DPDT	Double Pole Double Throw	This is equivalent to two SPDT switches controlled by a single mechanism.	
Crossbar	-	This is a switch connecting multiple inputs to multiple outputs in a matrix. The most famous use of these switches are in telephony and circuit switching.	

Integrated circuits

Integrated circuits, commonly referred to as IC, are electronics components that combine several electronics components to a perform-specific task. For example, to control the motor, you require a higher current signal than that of your circuit can provide. In this case, you need to create another circuit that amplifies the current to a certain level that it can drive the motors and that will be a lot of effort. Instead of that, you can use L293D motor driver IC, which does the same thing. You can get more information (such as which pin does what task, what input it takes, what output it can provide, and so on) about a particular IC by reading its datasheets. Don't worry if at this moment it does not make that much sense, you will understand this better in the later part of this chapter. Integrated circuits come in different packaging. Typically the **Dual In-Line Package (DIC)** IC symbol is used, which is shown in the *Common Electronics Components* table.

Sensors

In electronics term, a sensor is a device that measures the quantity in the physical world and converts it into a format that is readable by an electronic instrument. The touchscreen of a mobile will be the best example of sensor that takes the input in the physical world from a user and converts it into a format that will be understood by the processor. A sensor's sensitivity indicates how much the sensor's output changes when the measured physical world quantity changes.

LCD

As you know, LCD stands for liquid crystal display. However, in electronics, you will be using a different LCD. In the later part of this chapter, you will be using 16*2 characters LCD JHD162A. 16*2 means in the JHD162A LCD, there will be 16 columns and 2 rows, which can be used to display 32 characters on the screen.

Wire

For connecting different electronics components in the prototype circuits, you will require connecting wire or hook up wire (you will see different terminology used at different places). This can be of two types: single-threaded and multi-threaded. From personal experience, I found it easy to work with a single-threaded wire than that of a multi-threaded wire.

Breadboard

Often you will require to test the prototype of the circuits that you have developed. Breadboard serves as a construction base for testing the electronics prototype. On breadboard, you can test your prototype without doing any kind of soldering just by connecting different components using wires. Have a look at this image to know how breadboard looks in the real world:

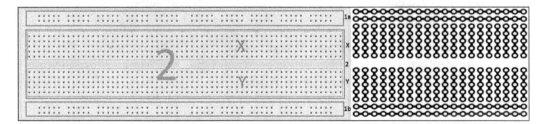

You will see two different sections (or areas called strips) in the breadboard:

- **Terminal strips**: This is the main area of the breadboard, which is generally used to hold most of the electronic components; this area is marked as area 2. As you can see in the following diagram, in this area, all the column are interconnected. The interesting part is that there is some space that divides this area into two subareas X and Y. This space is specifically designed for inserting **Integrated circuits (IC)** on the breadboard. So, when IC is plugged into a breadboard, the pins of one side will go to E, while the other side of pins will go to the F part:

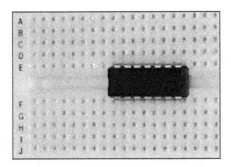

- **Bus strips**: The main use of a bus strip, which is marked as area *1a* and *1b*, is to provide power supply to the electronic components that are plugged-in on the terminal strips. Typically, there are two rows: one for ground and another one for a supply voltage. The first row is used to provide supply voltage and the second one to provide ground. A similar structure is available at the bottom of the breadboard to provide power supply and ground to the bottom part of the breadboard electronics component, where providing power supply and ground from the top part would be difficult in some cases.

A full-size terminal breadboard typically consists of around 56 to 65 columns of terminal strips, each column containing the two sets of connected clips (A to E and F to J), as mentioned earlier. Together with bus strips on each side, this makes up a typical 784 to 910 tie point/holes.

There are other electronics components that will be used in this book, but for now, the preceding information will help you get started. Other electronics components will get introduced to you as and when it is used.

Here's a table that shows you the common electronics components:

Electronic component	Symbol
Resistor	
Diodes	
Light Emitting Diode	
Integrated Circuits	
LCD	

Raspberry Pi electronics

Before this chapter, you have used Raspberry Pi as a web server, developed games, and created OS for it, but till this point, you haven't interacted much with the other parts of the development board. This section will take you on a tour of important electronics components/interfaces that will be used in this book.

There are four electronics components on Raspberry Pi that you need to understand, namely **P1**, **P2**, **P3**, **S2**, and **S5**:

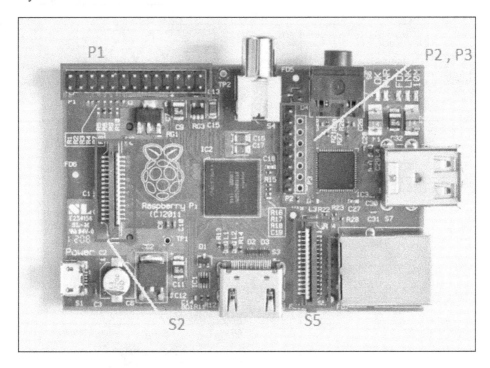

P1: This is commonly referred to as the GPIO connector. The GPIO connector actually has a number of different types of connections on them. They are:

- True **General-purpose input/output (GPIO)** pins that you can use to turn LEDs on and off and so on.

- **Inter-Integrated Circuits (I2C)** interface pins that allow you to connect low-speed hardware modules with just two control pins

- **Serial Peripheral Interface (SPI)**, which is an interface with SPI devices, a similar concept to I2C but a different standard

- Serial Rx and Tx pins for communication with serial peripherals

In the following image, Raspberry Pi pin numbers are shown. However, the Broadcom (the processor that is being used in Raspberry Pi) GPIO pin numbers are different than what is shown in the preceding image. So, mapping of pins as well as their functionality is displayed in the following table:

Broadcom chip numbers and functionality	Pin number	Pin number	Broadcom chip numbers and functionality
3.3 V	1	2	5 V
GPIO 0 (SDA) : (Rev. 2) GPIO 2	3	4	5 V
GPIO 1 (SLA) : (Rev. 2) GPIO 3	5	6	GND
GPIO 4	7	8	GPIO 14(TXD)
GND	9	10	GPIO 15(RXD)
GPIO 17	11	12	GPIO 18
GPIO 21 : (Rev. 2) GPIO 27	13	14	GND
GPIO 22	15	16	GPIO 23
3.3 V	17	18	GPIO 24
GPIO 10 (MOSI)	19	20	GND
GPIO 9 (MISO)	21	22	GPIO 25
GPIO 11 (SCKL)	23	24	GPIO 8
GND	25	26	GPIO 7

 In this book, the Raspberry Pi Model B board revision 1.0 is used. Model B board revision 2.0 has some changes in pin numbers. Those changes are also included in the preceding table.

As you can see in the previous table, you can use Pin 3 and Pin 5 for I2C, Pin 19, Pin 21, and Pin 23 for SPI to connect to SPI devices and Pin 8 and Pin 10 for UART communication. Right now, you don't have to worry about I2C, SPI, and UART; just bookmark this page, as it will be required when you want to program/control the device that is connected to one of this GPIO ports. For example, to change Pin 16 of the GPIO to HIGH, you have to use GPIO 23 to do the same.

P2 & P3: The P2 header is the VideoCore JTAG and used only during the production of the board. This cannot be used as the ARM JTAG. This connector is unpopulated in revision 2.0 boards. The P3 header, unpopulated, is the LAN9512 JTAG.

Some useful P2 and P3 pins are as follows:

Useful P2 pins	Useful P3 pins
Pin 1 - 3.3 V	Pin 7 - GND
Pin 7 – GND	-
Pin 8 – GND	-

S2 & S5: S2, the display serial interface, or DSI, is a high speed serial connector located between the power connector and the GPIO header on Raspberry Pi. The purpose of the DSI connector is to give the end user a quick and easy way to connect an LCD panel to the Pi. However, mostly, the HDMI port is used to connect with an LCD. S5 is the camera serial interface that can be used for connecting camera devices with Raspberry Pi. In 2013, a compatible 5 Megapixels and 1080p video resolutions camera was launched by Raspberry Pi.

WiringPi

As discussed in the earlier section, Raspberry Pi has 26 GPIO pins. These pins can be accessed/programmed using the WiringPi library, which is written in C for the BCM2835 processor used in Raspberry Pi. This is usable from C, C++, and many other languages using a suitable wrapper. In this book, the WiringPi Python wrapper is used.

Developing a digital clock

Having understood quite a bit of theory about electronic basics, Raspberry Pi electronics and understanding of the components, you are now ready to take your Raspberry Pi to the real world. Make sure you have all the components listed for you to go ahead:

- Raspberry Pi with Raspbian OS.

- A keyboard/mouse.

- A monitor to display the content of Raspberry Pi. If you don't have Raspberry Pi, you can install the VNC server on Raspberry Pi, and on your laptop using the VNC viewer, you will be able to display the content install VNC Server using an installation procedure described in *Chapter 1*, *Getting Started with Raspberry Pi*.

- Hook up wires of different colors (keep around 30 wires of around 10 cm long). To do: Read instructions on how to cut the wires.

- An HD44780-based LCD. Note; I have used JHD162A.

- A breadboard.

- 10K potentiometer (optional). You will be using potentiometer to control the contrast of the LCD, so if you don't have potentiometer, contrast would be fixed and that would be okay for this project.

Potentiometer is just a fancy word used for variable resistor. Basically, it is just a three-terminal resistor with sliding or rotating contact, which is used for changing the value of the resistor.

Setting up Raspberry Pi

Once you have all the components listed in the previous section, before you get started, there are some software installation that needs to be done:

```
Sudo apt-get update
```

For controlling GPIO pins of Raspberry Pi, you will be using Python so for that `python-dev`, `python-setuptools`, and `rpi.gpio` (the Python wrapper of WiringPi) are required. Install them using the following command:

```
Sudo apt-get install python-dev
Sudo apt-get install python-setuptools
Sudo apt-get install rpi.gpio
```

Now, your Raspberry Pi is all set to control the LCD, but before you go ahead and start connecting LCD pins with Raspberry Pi GPIO pins, you need to understand how LCD works and more specifically how HD44780 based LCD works.

Understanding HD44780-based LCD

The LCD character displays can be found in espresso machines, laser printers, children's toys, and maybe even the odd toaster. The Hitachi HD44780 controller has become an industry standard for these types of displays. If you look at the back side of the LCD that you have bought, you will find 16 pins:

Vcc / HIGH / '1'	+5 V
GND / LOW / '0'	0 V

The following table depicts the HD44780 pin number and functionality:

Pin number	Functionality
1	Ground
2	VCC
3	Contrast adjustment
4	Register select
5	Read/Write(R/W)

Pin number	Functionality
6	Clock(Enable)
7	Bit 0
8	Bit 1
9	Bit 2
10	Bit 3
11	Bit 4
12	Bit 5
13	Bit 6
14	Bit 7
15	Backlight anode (+)
16	Backlight cathode (-)

Pin 1 and Pin 2 are the power supply pins. They need to be connected with ground and +5 V power supply respectively.

Pin 3 is a contrast setting pin. It should be connected to a potentiometer to control the contrast. However, in a JHD162A LCD, if you directly connect this pin to ground, initially, you will see dark boxes but that will work if you don't have potentiometer.

Pin 4, Pin 5, and Pin 6 are the control pins.

Pin 7 to Pin 14 are the data pins of LCD. Pin 7 is the least significant bit and pin 14 is the most significant bit of the date inputs. You can use LCD in two modes, that is, 4-bit or 8-bit. In the next section, you will be doing 4-bit operation to control the LCD. If you want to display some number/character on the display, you have to input the appropriate codes for that number/character on these pins.

Pin 15 and Pin 16 provide power supply to the backlight of LCD. A backlight is a light within the LCD panel, which makes seeing the characters on the screen easier. When you leave your cell phone or MP3 player untouched for some time, the screen goes dark. This is the backlight turning off. It is possible to use the LCD without the backlight as well. JHD162A has a backlight, so you need to connect the power supply and ground to these pins respectively.

Pin 4, Pin 5, and Pin 6 are the most important pins. As mentioned in the table, Pin 4 is the register select pin. This allows you to switch between two operating modes of the LCD, namely the instruction and character modes. Depending on the status of this pin, the data on the 8 data pins (D0-D7) is treated as either an instruction or as character data. To display some characters on LCD, you have to activate the character mode. And to give some instructions such as "clear the display" and "move cursor to home", you have to activate the command mode. To set the LCD in the instruction mode, set Pin 4 to '0' and to put it in character mode, set Pin 4 to '1'. Mostly, you will be using the LCD to display something on the screen; however, sometimes you may require to read what is being written on the LCD. In this case, Pin 5 (read-write) is used. If you set Pin 5 to 0, it will work in the write mode, and if you set Pin 5 to 1, it will work in the read mode. For all the practical purposes, Pin 5 (R/W) has to be permanently set to 0, that is, connect it with GND (Ground). Pin 6 (enable pin) has a very simple function. This is just the clock input for the LCD. The instruction or the character data at the data pins (Pin 7-Pin 14) is processed by the LCD on the falling edge of this pin. The enable pin should be normally held at 1, that is, Vcc by a pull up resistor. When a momentary button switch is pressed, the pin goes low and back to high again when you leave the switch. Your instruction or character will be executed on the falling edge of the pulse, that is, the moment when the switch get closed.

So, the flow diagram of a typical write sequence to LCD will be:

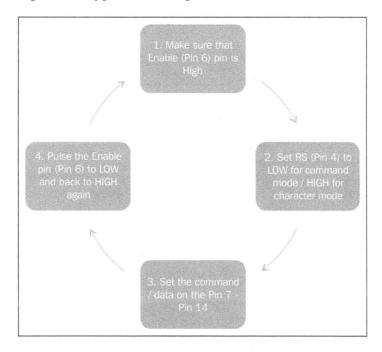

Connecting LCD pins and Raspberry Pi GPIO pins

Having understood the way LCD works, you are ready to connect your LCD with Raspberry Pi. Connect LCD pins with Raspberry Pi pins using following table:

LCD pins	Functionality	Raspberry Pi pins
1	Ground	Pin 6
2	Vcc	Pin 2
3	Contrast adjustment	Pin 6
4	Register select	Pin 26
5	Read/Write (R/W)	Pin 6
6	Clock (Enable)	Pin 24
7	Bit 0	Not used
8	Bit 1	Not used
9	Bit 2	Not used
10	Bit 3	Not used
11	Bit 4	Pin 22
12	Bit 5	Pin 18
13	Bit 6	Pin 16
14	Bit 7	Pin 12
15	Backlight anode (+)	Pin 2
16	Backlight cathode (-)	Pin 6

Your LCD should have come with 16-pin single row pin header (male/female) soldered with 16 pins of LCD. If you didn't get any pin header with the LCD, you have to buy a 16-pin single row female pin header. If the LCD that you bought doesn't have a soldered 16-pin single row pin header, you have to solder it. Please note that if you have not done soldering before, don't try to solder it by yourself. Ask some of your friends who can help or the easiest option is to take it to the place from where you have bought it; he will solder it for you in merely 5 minutes.

The final connections are shown in the following screenshot. Make sure your Raspberry Pi is not running when you are connecting LCD pins with Raspberry Pi pins. Connect LCD pins with Raspberry Pi using hook up wires.

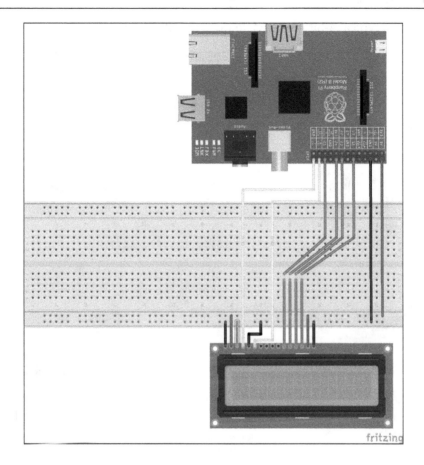

Before you start scripting, you need to understand few more things about operating LCD in a 4-bit mode:

- LCD default is a 8-bit mode, so the first command must be set in a 8-bit mode instructing the LCD to operate in a 4-bit mode

- In the 4-bit mode, a write sequence is a bit different than what has been depicted earlier for the 8-bit mode. In the following diagram, Step 3 will be different in the 4-bit mode as there are only 4 data pins available for data transfer and you cannot transfer 8 bits at the same time. So in this case, as per the HD44780 datasheet, you have to send the first **Upper "nibble"** to LCD Pin 11 to Pin 14. Execute those bits by making **Enable pin to LOW** (as instructions/character will get executed on the falling edge of the pulse) and back to HIGH again. Once you have sent the **Upper "nibble"**, send **Lower "nibble"** to LCD Pin 11 to Pin 14. To execute the instruction/ character sent, set **Enable Pin to LOW**.

So, the typical 4-bit mode write process will look like this:

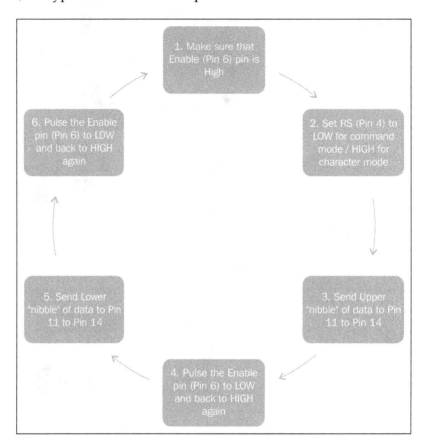

Scripting

Once you have connected LCD pins with Raspberry Pi, as per the previously shown diagram, boot up your Raspberry Pi. The following are the steps to develop a digital clock:

1. Create a new python script by right-clicking **Create | New File |** DigitalClock.py.

    Here is the code that needs to be copied in the DigitalClock.py file:

    ```
    #!/usr/bin/python
    import RPi.GPIO as GPIO
    import time
    from time import sleep
    from datetime import datetime
    ```

```python
from time import strftime
class HD44780:
  def __init__(self, pin_rs=7, pin_e=8,
  pins_db=[18,23,24,25]):
   self.pin_rs=pin_rs
    self.pin_e=pin_e
    self.pins_db=pins_db
    GPIO.setmode(GPIO.BCM)
    GPIO.setup(self.pin_e, GPIO.OUT)
    GPIO.setup(self.pin_rs, GPIO.OUT)
    for pin in self.pins_db:
      GPIO.setup(pin, GPIO.OUT)
      self.clear()
  def clear(self):
    # Blank / Reset LCD
    self.cmd(0x33)
    self.cmd(0x32)
    self.cmd(0x28)
    self.cmd(0x0C)
    self.cmd(0x06)
    self.cmd(0x01)
  def cmd(self, bits, char_mode=False):
    # Send command to LCD
    sleep(0.001)
    bits=bin(bits)[2:].zfill(8)
    GPIO.output(self.pin_rs, char_mode)
    for pin in self.pins_db:
      GPIO.output(pin, False)
    for i in range(4):
      if bits[i] == "1":
        GPIO.output(self.pins_db[i], True)
    GPIO.output(self.pin_e, True)
    GPIO.output(self.pin_e, False)
    for pin in self.pins_db:
      GPIO.output(pin, False)
    for i in range(4,8):
      if bits[i] == "1":
        GPIO.output(self.pins_db[i-4], True)
GPIO.output(self.pin_e, True)
    GPIO.output(self.pin_e, False)
  def message(self, text):
    # Send string to LCD. Newline wraps to second line
    for char in text:
      if char == '\n':
```

```
                self.cmd(0xC0) # next line
            else:
                self.cmd(ord(char),True)
    if __name__ == '__main__':
        while True:
            lcd = HD44780()
            lcd.message(" "+datetime.now().strftime(%H:%M:%S))
        time.sleep(1)
```

2. Run the preceding script by executing the following command:

   sudo python DigitalClock.py

   This code accesses the Raspberry Pi GPIO port, which requires root privileges, so sudo is used.

3. Now, your digital clock is ready. The current Raspberry Pi time will get displayed on the LCD screen.

Only 4 data pins of LCD are being connected, so this script will work for the LCD 4-bit mode.

> I have used the JHD162A LCD, which is based on the HD44780 controller. Controlling mechanisms for all HD44780 LCDs are same. So, the preceding class, HD44780, can also be used for controlling another HD44780-based LCD. Moreover, you will reuse the same class in next section as well.

Once you have understood the preceding LCD 4-bit operation, it will be much easier to understand this code:

```
if __name__ == '__main__':
    while True:
        lcd = HD44780()
        lcd.message(" "+datetime.now().strftime(%H:%M:%S))
    time.sleep(1)
```

The main HD44780 class has been initialized and the current time will be sent to the LCD every one second by calling the message function of the lcd object. The most important part of this project is the HD44780 class.

The HD44780 class has the following four components:

- __init__: This will initialize the necessary components.
- clear: This will clear the LCD and instruct it to work in the 4-bit mode.

- `cmd`: This is the core of the class. Each and every command/instruction that has to be executed will get executed in this function.

- `message`: This will be used to display a message on the screen.

The __init__ function

The _init_ function initializes the necessary GPIO port for LCD operation:

```
def __init__(self, pin_rs=7, pin_e=8, pins_db=[18,23,24,25]):
  self.pin_rs=pin_rs
  self.pin_e=pin_e
  self.pins_db=pins_db
  GPIO.setmode(GPIO.BCM)
  GPIO.setup(self.pin_e, GPIO.OUT)
  GPIO.setup(self.pin_rs, GPIO.OUT)
  for pin in self.pins_db:
    GPIO.setup(pin, GPIO.OUT)
    self.clear()
```

`GPIO.setmode(GPIO.BCM)`: Basically, the GPIO library has two modes in which it can operate. One is BOARD and the other one is BCM. The BOARD mode specifies that you are referring to the numbers printed in the board. The BCM mode means that you are referring to the pins by the "Broadcom SOC channel" number. The *Mapping of LCD pins and Raspberry Pi pins* table shows the mapping between BOARD pins and BCM pins. While creating an instance of the HD44780 class, you can specify which pin to use for a specific purpose. By default, it will take GPIO 7 as RS Pin, GPIO 8 as Enable Pin, and GPIO 18, GPIO 23, GPIO 24, and GPIO 25 as data pins. Once you have defined the mode of the GPIO operation, you have to set all the pins that will be used as output, as you are going to provide output of these pins to LCD pins. Once this is done, clear and initialize the screen.

The clear function

The clear function clears/resets the LCD:

```
def clear(self):
  # Blank / Reset LCD
  self.cmd(0x33)
  self.cmd(0x32)
  self.cmd(0x28)
  self.cmd(0x0C)
  self.cmd(0x06)
  self.cmd(0x01)
```

You will see some code sequence that is executed in this section. This code sequence is generated based on the HD44780 datasheet instructions. A complete discussion of this code is beyond the scope of this book; however, to give a high-level overview, the functionality of each code is as follows:

- 0x33: This is the function set to the 8-bit mode
- 0x32: This is the function set to the 8-bit mode again
- 0x28: This is the function set to the 4-bit mode, which indicates the LCD has two lines
- 0x0C: This turns on just the LCD and not the cursor
- 0x06: This sets the entry mode to the autoincrement cursor and disables the shift mode
- 0x01: This clears the display

The cmd function

The cmd function sends the command to the LCD as per the LCD operation explained in the earlier section, and is shown as follows:

```
def cmd(self, bits, char_mode=False):
  # Send command to LCD
  sleep(0.001)
  bits=bin(bits)[2:].zfill(8)
  GPIO.output(self.pin_rs, char_mode)
  for pin in self.pins_db:
    GPIO.output(pin, False)
  for i in range(4):
   if bits[i] == "1":
      GPIO.output(self.pins_db[i], True)
  GPIO.output(self.pin_e, True)
  GPIO.output(self.pin_e, False)
  for pin in self.pins_db:
    GPIO.output(pin, False)
  for i in range(4,8):
    if bits[i] == "1":
      GPIO.output(self.pins_db[i-4], True)
  GPIO.output(self.pin_e, True)
  GPIO.output(self.pin_e, False)
```

As the 4-bit mode is used drive the LCD, you will be using the flowchart that has been discussed previously. In the first line, the sleep(0.001) second is used because a few LCD operations will take some time to execute, so you have to wait for a certain time before it gets completed. The bits=bin(bits)[2:].zfill(8) line will convert the integer number to binary string and then pad it with zeros on the left to make it proper 8-bit data that can be sent to the LCD processor. The preceding lines of code does the operation as per the 4-bit write operation flowchart.

The message function

The message function sends the string to LCD, as shown here:

```
def message(self, text):
  # Send string to LCD. Newline wraps to second line
  for char in text:
    if char == '\n':
      self.cmd(0xC0) # next line
    else:
      self.cmd(ord(char),True)
```

This function will take the string as input, convert each character into the corresponding ASCII code, and then send it to the cmd function. For a new line, the 0xC0 code is used.

Developing an e-mail notifier

This section is an extension of the digital clock that you have developed in the previous section. In addition to all the components mentioned in the previous section, you will require one green LED and one red LED for displaying the status. In this section, you will develop an e-mail notifier, which will turn red if you have any unread e-mails and it will turn green if you have no unread e-mails. This will also show the count of unread messages on the LCD by using the code that you have developed in the previous section.

Connecting LCD pins and Raspberry Pi GPIO pins

As this is an extension of the previous section, first make sure you have connected the LCD pins and Raspberry GPIO pins as mentioned previously. In addition to the connection you have made, you have to connect two LEDs at Raspberry Pi Pin 14 and Pin 15. Connect the anode of the green LED and red LED to Pin 14 and Pin 15 respectively. Similarly, connect the cathode of both LEDs to GND. Complete the connection diagram, as shown here:

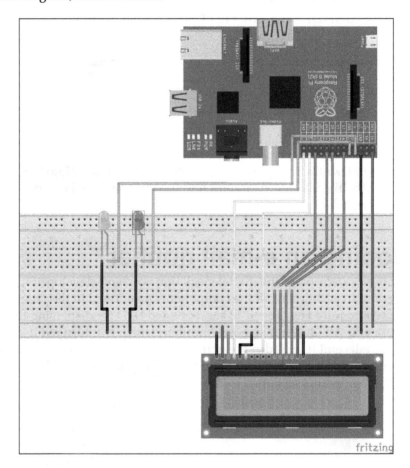

Scripting

Once you have connected the Raspberry Pi pins with LCD pins and LED pins, create a new file as EmailNotifier.py.

Here is the code that needs to be copied in the `EmailNotifier.py` file:

```python
#!/usr/bin/python
import threading , feedparser, time
import RPi.GPIO as GPIO
from time import strftime
from datetime import datetime
from time import sleep
USERNAME = "username"       # just the part before the @ sign, add
yours here
PASSWORD = "password"

GREEN_LED = 14
RED_LED = 15

class HD44780:

  def __init__(self, pin_rs=7, pin_e=8, pins_db=[18,23,24,25]):
    self.pin_rs=pin_rs
    self.pin_e=pin_e
    self.pins_db=pins_db

    GPIO.setmode(GPIO.BCM)
    GPIO.setup(self.pin_e, GPIO.OUT)
    GPIO.setup(self.pin_rs, GPIO.OUT)
   GPIO.setup(GREEN_LED, GPIO.OUT)
   GPIO.setup(RED_LED, GPIO.OUT)
    for pin in self.pins_db:
      GPIO.setup(pin, GPIO.OUT)

    self.clear()

  def clear(self):
    # Blank / Reset LCD """

    self.cmd(0x33)
    self.cmd(0x32)
    self.cmd(0x28)
    self.cmd(0x0C)
    self.cmd(0x06)
    self.cmd(0x01)

  def cmd(self, bits, char_mode=False):
```

```python
        # Send command to LCD """

        sleep(0.001)
        bits=bin(bits)[2:].zfill(8)

        GPIO.output(self.pin_rs, char_mode)

        for pin in self.pins_db:
            GPIO.output(pin, False)

        for i in range(4):
            if bits[i] == "1":
                GPIO.output(self.pins_db[i], True)

        GPIO.output(self.pin_e, True)
        GPIO.output(self.pin_e, False)

        for pin in self.pins_db:
            GPIO.output(pin, False)

        for i in range(4,8):
            if bits[i] == "1":
                GPIO.output(self.pins_db[i-4], True)

        GPIO.output(self.pin_e, True)
        GPIO.output(self.pin_e, False)

    def message(self, text="' '+datetime.now().strftime('%H:%M:%S')"):
        # Send string to LCD. Newline wraps to second line"""

        for char in text:
            if char == '\n':
                self.cmd(0xC0) # next line
            else:
                self.cmd(ord(char),True)

if __name__=='__main__':

    while True:
        lcd = HD44780()
        newmails = int(feedparser.parse("https://" + USERNAME + ":" +
        PASSWORD +"@mail.google.com/gmail/feed/atom")["feed"]
["fullcount"])
```

```
   print "You have", newmails, "new emails!"
   lcd.message(" You have "+ str(newmails) +" \n mails .")
if newmails> 0:
   GPIO.output(GREEN_LED, True)
   GPIO.output(RED_LED, False)
   print 'Green'
else:
   GPIO.output(GREEN_LED, False)
   GPIO.output(RED_LED, True)
   print 'red'

time.sleep(60)
```

Copy the preceding code in the EmailNotifier.py file and then run it using the following command:

```
sudo python EmailNotifier.py
```

As mentioned earlier, this is an extension of the previous project, so you already have the understanding of HD44780 class, which is given as follows:

```
if __name__=='__main__':
   while True:
      lcd = HD44780()
      newmails = int(feedparser.parse("https://" + USERNAME + ":" +
      PASSWORD +"@mail.google.com/gmail/feed/atom")
      ["feed"]["fullcount"])

      print "You have", newmails, "new emails!"
      lcd.message(" You have "+ str(newmails) +" \n mails .")
        if newmails> 0:
      GPIO.output(GREEN_LED, True)
      GPIO.output(RED_LED, False)
      print 'Green'
   else:
      GPIO.output(GREEN_LED, False)
      GPIO.output(RED_LED, True)
      print 'red'
   time.sleep(60)
```

There are two additions in this section:

- The feedparser library is used for reading data from the Gmail server
- Two LEDs, red and green, are connected for showing the status of unread e-mails

This will also show the count of unread e-mails on the LCD. If the user has 0 unread e-mails, then the green LED will turn ON by sending `True` to `GREEN_LED` and sending `False` to `RED_LED`; otherwise, the red LED will remain ON. It will check the status of unread e-mail every single minute. One minute difference between each execution has been introduced using the `time.sleep(60)` command.

Developing an alarm clock

After developing two projects, you must be confident working with Raspberry Pi GPIO, LED and LCD. In this section, apart from a little bit of more coding, you will be using one or more pieces of hardware, which is a speaker with Raspberry Pi. You will develop an alarm clock that will be turned on at specific time set by the user and it will turn off only when the user answers two simple mathematical questions correctly. Similar to the previous section, in this section, you will be reusing the LCD code that was developed in the digital clock section.

Connecting LCD pins, Raspberry Pi GPIO pins, and a speaker

As this is an extension of a digital clock section, first make sure that you have connected the LCD pins and Raspberry GPIO pins, as mentioned in the following screenshot. In addition to the connection that you have made, you have to connect the speaker with the 3.5 mm audio jack of Raspberry Pi.

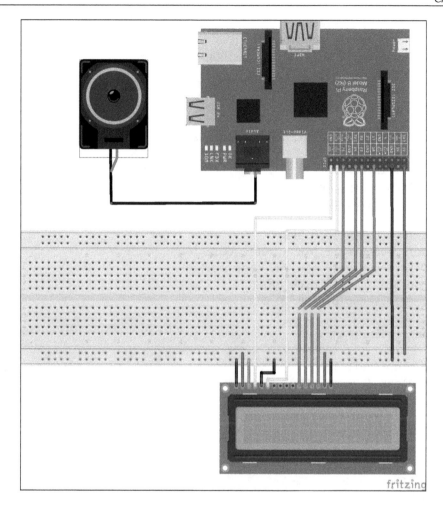

Scripting

Once you have connected all the components as per the connection diagram, create a new file as AlarmClock.py:

```python
#!/usr/bin/python
import time
import os
import threading , feedparser, time
import RPi.GPIO as GPIO
from time import strftime
from datetime import datetime
```

```python
from time import sleep
from random import randint
import subprocess
import sys

class HD44780:

  def __init__(self, pin_rs=7, pin_e=8, pins_db=[18,23,24,25]):

    self.pin_rs=pin_rs
    self.pin_e=pin_e
    self.pins_db=pins_db

    GPIO.setmode(GPIO.BCM)
    GPIO.setup(self.pin_e, GPIO.OUT)
    GPIO.setup(self.pin_rs, GPIO.OUT)
    for pin in self.pins_db:
      GPIO.setup(pin, GPIO.OUT)

    self.clear()

  def clear(self):
    # Blank / Reset LCD

    self.cmd(0x33)
    self.cmd(0x32)
    self.cmd(0x28)
        self.cmd(0x0C)
    self.cmd(0x06)
    self.cmd(0x01)

  def cmd(self, bits, char_mode=False):
    # Send command to LCD

    sleep(0.001)
    bits=bin(bits)[2:].zfill(8)

    GPIO.output(self.pin_rs, char_mode)

    for pin in self.pins_db:
      GPIO.output(pin, False)

    for i in range(4):
```

```
    if bits[i] == "1":
       GPIO.output(self.pins_db[i], True)

  GPIO.output(self.pin_e, True)
  GPIO.output(self.pin_e, False)

  for pin in self.pins_db:
    GPIO.output(pin, False)

  for i in range(4,8):
    if bits[i] == "1":
       GPIO.output(self.pins_db[i-4], True)

  GPIO.output(self.pin_e, True)
  GPIO.output(self.pin_e, False)

  def message(self, text="'
  '+datetime.now().strftime('%H:%M:%S')")  :
    # Send string to LCD. Newline wraps to second line

    for char in text:
    if char == '\n':
      self.cmd(0xC0) # next line
    else:
      self.cmd(ord(char),True)

if __name__=='__main__':
  lcd = HD44780()
  lcd.message(" Enter Hour \n 24hr Format")
  alarm_HH = input("Enter the hour you want to wake up at: ")
  lcd.clear()
  lcd.message(" Enter Minute ")
     alarm_MM = input("Enter the minute you want to wake up at: ")
  lcd.clear()
  lcd.message(" Alarm set at \n "+str(alarm_HH)+":"+str(alarm_MM))
  print("Alarm Set at: {0:02}:{1:02}").format(alarm_HH, alarm_MM)
  hours=int(alarm_HH)
  minutes=int(alarm_MM)
  keep_running=True;

  while keep_running:
    now = time.localtime()
    if (now.tm_hour == hours and now.tm_min == minutes):
      print("ALARM NOW!\n")
```

```
        p=subprocess.Popen(['omxplayer
        AlarmClock.mp3'],stdin=subprocess.PIPE,shell=True)
            correctAnswerCount=0
        while True:
          number1=randint(0,9)
          number2=randint(10,19)
          lcd.clear()
          lcd.message(" "+str(number1)+" + "+str(number2))
              userInput=raw_input(str(number1)+"+"+str(number2))
          try:
            answer = int(userInput)
            if(answer==number1+number2):
              correctAnswerCount+=1
            if(correctAnswerCount==2):
              print "Alarm Off"
                  lcd.clear()
                  lcd.message(" Alarm Off ")
              keep_running=False
              p.communicate('q')
              os._exit(1)
          except ValueError:
            print("That's not an int!")
      else:
        time.sleep(60)
```

Copy the preceding code in the `AlarmClock.py` file and then run it using the following command:

sudo python AlarmClock.py

In this script, first you have to ask the user at what time he wants to set the alarm. Assuming the user doesn't have the HDMI screen to view what has been written on the screen, each message has to be displayed on the LCD. Once the user enters the hour and minute at which he wants to set the alarm, further processing will be done. This has been scripted using the following code:

```
  if __name__=='__main__':
    lcd = HD44780()
    lcd.message(" Enter Hour \n 24hr Format")
        alarm_HH = input("Enter the hour you want to wake up at: ")
    lcd.clear()
    lcd.message(" Enter Minute ")
    alarm_MM = input("Enter the minute you want to wake up at: ")
    lcd.clear()
    lcd.message(" Alarm set at \n "+str(alarm_HH)+":"+str(alarm_MM))
```

```
print("Alarm Set at: {0:02}:{1:02}").format(alarm_HH, alarm_MM)
hours=int(alarm_HH)
minutes=int(alarm_MM)
```

 If you don't clear the LCD before displaying new message, it will show the previous message.

Once you have the input from the user, you have to compare that with the current time till the current time matches the alarm time. As soon as the current time matches the alarm time, you have to play some sound file. Simple mathematical questions are generated using two random numbers. A user has to answer the sum of these two numbers. An alarm will be ON until the user provides two correct answers. If the user doesn't provide an input in the integer format, then the program should not terminate. To take care of this scenario, first convert the user input into integer, and if it is not integer, catch the exception and continue the execution:

```
keep_running=True;

while keep_running:
  now = time.localtime()
  if (now.tm_hour == hours and now.tm_min == minutes):
    print("ALARM NOW!\n")
    p=subprocess.Popen(['omxplayer AlarmClock.mp3'],
    stdin=subprocess.PIPE,shell=True)
    correctAnswerCount=0
    while True:
      number1=randint(0,9)
      number2=randint(10,19)
      lcd.clear()
      lcd.message(" "+str(number1)+" + "+str(number2))
      userInput=raw_input(str(number1)+"+"+str(number2))
      try:
        answer = int(userInput)
        if(answer==number1+number2):
          correctAnswerCount+=1
        if(correctAnswerCount==2):
          print "Alarm Off"
          lcd.clear()
          lcd.message(" Alarm Off ")
          keep_running=False
          p.communicate('q')
          os._exit(1)
      except ValueError:
```

```
        print("That's not an int!")
    else:
        time.sleep(60)
```

 You can download the sound files from the Internet or transfer some sound files from your computer to Raspberry Pi using USB a pendrive.

```
p=subprocess.Popen(['omxplayer
AlarmClock.mp3'],stdin=subprocess.PIPE,shell=True)
```

This line is a bit tricky. The subprocess module of Python provides a consistent interface to creating and working with additional processes. You have to create another process or else it will block the current program execution. What you want is as soon as an alarm is turned ON, sound should be played in the background and then the user will be asked simple mathematical questions. If the user answers two questions correctly, program execution will be stopped and it should also stop playing sound files. Omxplayer is already installed on Raspberry Pi, so you don't have to install anything to play the sound files. The `'omxplayer AlarmSound.mp3'` command will play the sound file. The `'stdin=subprocess.PIPE'` parameter is provided so that input for the main process and sound playing process is not merged. In other words, it will create another input channel for subprocess and input to the subprocess can be sent using the `p.communicate(INPUT)` command. As once user answers two questions correctly, you need to close the sound file and subprocess which is not directly accessible. The second parameter `shell=True` is required for closing the file from the shell. Omxplayer has command `'q'` for closing the file.

 To get all the commands for omxplayer in your terminal, write `omxplayer -k`.

So, using the `p.communicate('q')` command, you can close the sound file being played in the background by omxplayer. The `HD44780` class has already been discussed in the *Developing a digital clock* section.

Summary

In this chapter, basic laws of electronics have been introduced along with various electronics components. Raspberry Pi electronics and LCD basics have been covered at length, which helped in developing a digital clock, e-mail notifier, and alarm clock.

In the next chapter, a remote controlled robot will be developed. More complex electronics components will get introduced, and it will tie together everything that has been covered so far in this book.

4
Getting into Robotics

Robotics has become the buzz word of today's fast paced growing digital world. Robots are being used in every industry, be it in space, manufacturing, auto, or even in the medical industry. In the previous chapters, you learned about web servers, basics of electronics, and how to connect Raspberry Pi to the real world using the GPIO port. This chapter ties together everything that you have learned so far. Also, a few more electronics components will be introduced that are required to build your own robot. Once you have understood the electronic components, you will learn how to develop a remote-controlled robot that displays a real-time video feed from the Raspberry Pi camera and display the distance to a nearest object using an ultrasonic sensor. We will cover the following sections in this chapter:

- Introduction to robotics
- Few more electronic components
- Displaying a live feed from the Raspberry Pi camera module using a web server
- Developing a project that calculates the distance of Raspberry Pi to the nearest object using an ultrasonic sensor
- Develop a remote-controlled robot
- Develop a remote-controlled robot that shows the Raspberry Pi camera live feed and the distance of the robot to the nearest object in real time

Introduction to robotics

What is the first thing that comes to your mind when you think of robotics or robots? For many people, it is a machine that imitates the human-like Wall-E, but such robots still inhabit science fiction. People still aren't able to give robots enough intelligence, or what we commonly refer to as common sense, to reliably interact with the dynamic world. So, what exactly is a robot? This is a system that contains sensors, control systems, manipulators, power supplies, and software all working together to perform a task.

I would define a robot as any machine that simplifies our tasks/processes.

Robotics is a branch of physics, mechanical engineering, electrical engineering, structural engineering, mathematics, and computing that deals with the designing, building, programming, and testing of robots. Robot in Czech is a word for worker or servant. The word robot was coined by a Czech novelist Karel Capek in a 1920 play titled **Rassum's Universal Robots (RUR)**. In 1942, the science fiction written by Isaac Asimov formulated *Three Laws of Robotics* in his short story, *Runaround*:

- A robot may not injure a human being or, through inaction, allow a human being to come to harm

- A robot must obey the orders given to it by human beings, except where such orders would conflict with the first law

- A robot must protect its own existence as long as such protection does not conflict with the First or Second Law

Nowadays, robots do a lot of different tasks in many fields and the number of jobs entrusted to robots is growing rapidly. To understand where the robotic advancement is headed, have a look at Honda Asimo (`http://asimo.honda.com/`), which they claim to be the world's most advanced humanoid. Boston Dynamics (`http://www.bostondynamics.com/`), which was bought by Google in December, 2013, is one of the leading companies in robotics advancement. Nowadays, robots are becoming smarter and more personal; to give you an example, have a look at JIBO (`http://www.myjibo.com/`), which is the world's first family robot. JIBO's potential extends far beyond engaging in a casual conversation and completing daily tasks. Maybe one day, you will be able to make something similar of your own.

More electronic components

You are already one step closer to building your own robot as you already know the basics of electronics and have developed few applications using Raspberry Pi. To take further steps in this direction, in this chapter, you will learn how to develop a remote-controlled robot that will be able to live stream video over the Internet and also send distance of the nearest object in real time. Before you move ahead, you need to understand a few more electronics components:

- Introduction to motors
- Introduction to multimeter
- The robotic base
- The level converter

- Motor driver IC / H-Bridge
- The Raspberry Pi camera
- An ultrasonic sensor
- The Raspberry Pi battery
- The Raspberry Pi WiFi module

Introduction to motors

As mentioned earlier, in this chapter, you will develop a remote-controlled robot with some add-on features, so the first thing that you need to make a robot movable are wheels. Now, once you got the wheels, you need some mechanism that can control the speed of the wheels. Motors are used for this purpose; they convert electrical energy into mechanical energy. A world without electric motors is difficult to imagine. From the tiniest motor found in a quartz watch to a million-plus horsepower motor powering a ship, motors are used in many diverse applications. The following screenshot is an example of a motor:

There are basically two types of conventional electrical motor available: AC type motors and DC type motors. AC motors are generally used in high power single or multi-phase industrial applications, where a constant rotational torque and speed is required to control large loads such as fans or pumps. DC motors are used in many electronics, positional control, microprocessor, PIC, and robotic circuits. Another DC motors that is commonly used in robotics is the stepper motor. This is particularly well suited to applications that require accurate positioning and a fast response to starting, stopping, reversing, and speed control. Another key feature of the stepper motor is its ability to hold the load steady once the required position is achieved. For example, in a normal DC motor, once you stopped the power to motor, it will still go to some distance because of the continuous motion, while in a stepper motor, once you stop the power, it will stop instantaneously.

[There are many other DC motors as well, but discussion of all motors is out of the scope for this book. In this book, you will be using a normal DC motor.]

Introduction to multimeter

A multimeter is an electronic measuring instrument that combines several measurement functions in one unit. A typical multimeter can include features such as the ability to measure voltage, current, and resistance. It is also known as a **volt-ohm meter** (**VOM**). It can be of two types: analog multimeter and digital multimeter based on the circuit used in the construction. An analog multimeter usually shows results using a pointer that moves over a scale calibrated for all the different measurements that can be made, while on the digital multimeter digits are displayed on the screen. A typical digital multimeter is shown in the following image:

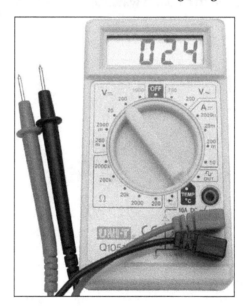

A typical analog multimeter is shown in the following image:

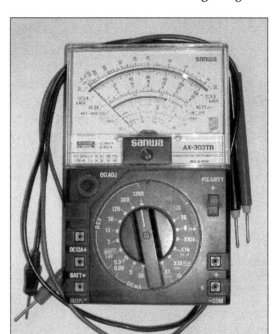

Most of the time, you will be using digital multimeter, so you need to understand the capabilities and usage of digital multimeter. On the bottom-right corner of the multimeter, you will see three holes where you can connect a measuring cable. If your circuit operates on higher currents, connect the anode (typically a red probe) to the first hole and connect the cathode (typically, a black probe) to the last hole. The second hole is for circuits operating at low current. Most of the time, you will be using the second hole, where you will connect the anode (typically, a red probe) and the third hole, where you will connect the cathode (typically, a black probe). Here are some features that you will be using while developing a robot in this chapter:

- **Section A**: This is for measuring DC voltage. It can measure voltage in a different range. For example, the multimeter shown in the preceding figure can measure voltage up to 1000V.

- **Section B**: This is for measuring resistance. While we can calculate the resistance of the resistor using the color code described in *Chapter 3*, *Introduction to Electronics*, using multimeter you can quickly measure the resistance. It can measure resistance in different ranges. For example, the multimeter shown in the preceding picture can measure resistance up to 2000K Ohm.

- **Section C** and **Section D**: These features are used for measuring AC voltage and AC current respectively. You will rarely use these functionalities as electronics components work on DC voltage and current.

- **Section E**: As a beginner, you will be using this section more often. This section is to check the continuity in the circuit. In any electronics circuit that you will develop, the first thing that you should do if your circuit doesn't work is to check the continuity in the circuit. Connect anode and cathode of the multimeter to the circuit across which you want to test the continuity. This will beep when circuit conducts.

- **Other**: Additionally, some multimeters can also measure temperature in degrees Celsius or Fahrenheit, with an appropriate temperature test probe, often a thermocouple.

Robotic base

Once you have the motors for the movement, you need some kind of base that can hold all the motors at a certain distance for the proper movement of the robot. Apart from holding the motor, you need some firm base on which you can place all the electronics components. In this chapter, you will build a 4-wheel robot, so you will require a 4-wheel robotic base. You will be able to get it from a nearby electronics shop. Have a look at the following image to get a clear idea of how it will look in the real world:

Level converter

Because most of the electronics power supply provide 5V and most modern sensors displays are 3.3V only, you need to perform level shifting/conversion to protect the 3.3V device from 5V. Although you can use resistors to make a simple divider, for high-speed transfers, the resistors cause a havoc that is tough to debug. For this reason, you have to use a level converter. Those converters can be of two types: unidirectional and bi-directional. As the name suggests, a unidirectional converter can only convert in one direction, that is, either from 5V to 3.3V or 3.3V to 5V. While on the other end, a bi-directional converter can convert 5V to 3.3V as well as 3.3V to 5V.

> Later in this book, you will use a resistor divider circuit to step down the 5V to 3.3V.

Motor driver IC

Depending on the DC motor used, it requires voltage varying from 5V to 36V. Raspberry Pi GPIO can't provide such high range of voltage, so you need some kind of level converter. Moreover, you need to drive the motor in both directions, so some special circuitry is required for this purpose. That special circuit is embedded in a typically used motor driver L293D IC. It works on the concept of H-bridge. Before you understand the functionality of L293D, you need to understand what is H-bridge and the basic functionality of the H-bridge circuit.

H-Bridge

H-Bridge is an electronic circuit that enables the voltage to be applied across a motor (in general, any load) in both directions. It can be built using four switches. The following diagram shows the basic structure of an H-bridge:

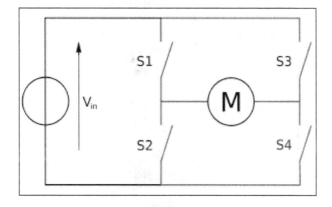

Generally, it is used to change the direction of the motor, but it can also be used for other two purposes:

- "Brake" the motor: When the motor terminals are shortened, it will come to a sudden stop

- "Free run" the motor: When the motor terminals are disconnected from a circuit, it will free run to a point

S1	S2	S3	S4	Result
Close	Open	Open	Close	The motor moves right
Open	Close	Close	Open	The motor moves left
Open	Open	Open	Open	The motor free runs
Open	Close	Open	Close	The motor brakes
Close	Open	Close	Open	The motor brakes
Close	Close	Open	Open	Shoot-through
Open	Open	Close	Close	Shoot-through
Close	Close	Close	Close	Shoot-through

In the preceding table, you can see there is one more condition "Shoot-through". When the power supply gets directly shorted, it is called "Shoot-through". You should never use these conditions in your circuits.

Motor driver IC L293D has two H-bridge circuits, so you can control a set of two DC motors simultaneously in any direction. This is a 16-pin dual H-bridge motor driver integrated circuit. Due to its small size, it is widely used in robotics applications to control the DC motors. The pin diagram of the L293D IC is shown in the following diagram:

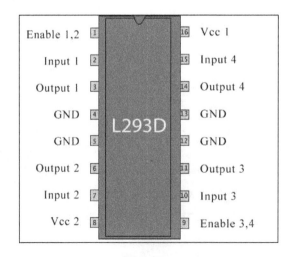

- **Enable Pins**: Pin 1 and Pin 9 enable pins. Both pins need to be HIGH if you want to use both H-bridge of the IC. For driving the motor with left H-bridge, you need to enable Pin 1 to HIGH. Similarly, to drive the motor with right H-bridge, you need to enable Pin 9 to HIGH. If one of the Pin 1 or Pin 9 goes low, then the motor in the corresponding section will suspend working.

- **Power Supply**: Pin 16 is an internal power supply pin where you need to connect 5V power supply. Pin 8 is for motor supply. Depending on the motor used, you can connect corresponding power supply required for that motor to Pin 8. ADD MORE DETAILS

- **Output Pins**: As mentioned before, L293D can drive two DC motors simultaneously. One motor should be connected to Pin 3 and Pin 6. Similarly, another motor can be connected to Pin 11 and Pin 14.

- **Ground Pins**: Pin 4, Pin 5, Pin 12, and Pin 13 are ground pins. These pins should be connected to GROUND/LOW.

- **Input Pins**: There are four input pins on the IC. Pin 2 and Pin 7 are for regulating the motor connected to the left side of the IC, and similarly, Pin 10 and Pin 15 are for regulating the motor connected to the right side of the IC. The motors are rotated based on the input provided across these inputs.

The following table shows the inputs provided and the corresponding result:

Pin 2 / Pin 15	Pin 7 / Pin 10	Result
HIGH	LOW	The motor moves in clockwise direction
LOW	HIGH	The motor moves in anticlockwise direction
LOW	LOW	No rotation
HIGH	HIGH	No rotation

The Raspberry Pi camera

Since the launch of Raspberry Pi board A, people all around the world are exploring it in numerous ways. Computer scientists and researchers have explored the USB camera with Raspberry Pi. However, not all the USB cameras are supported with Raspberry Pi, so Raspberry Pi foundation decided to build a camera module that can directly connect with the Raspberry Pi CSI connector. The 5MP camera module is capable of capturing 1080p video and still images. The module is around 25mm*20mm*9mm and weighs just over 3 gm, which makes it perfect for mobile or other applications where size and weight play an important role.

Setting up the camera

As mentioned earlier, before powering up the Raspberry Pi, connect the Raspberry Pi camera module to the board using CSI connector. The following steps will help you set up the camera:

1. Now, you have connected the hardware module to the Raspberry Pi. Before you can start taking photos using camera module, there are some software installation that needs to be done with the following commands:

   ```
   sudo apt-get update
   sudo apt-get install python-picamera
   ```

   `python-picamera` is a pure Python interface to the Raspberry Pi camera module for Python 2.7 and above. The `python3` package can be installed using the following command:

   ```
   sudo apt-get update
   sudo apt-get install python3-picamera
   ```

2. Before you start using the camera module, you need to enable the camera in the Raspberry Pi configuration file.

   Open the `raspi-config` tool from the terminal:

   ```
   sudo raspi-config
   ```

   Select the **Enable** camera and hit *Enter*, then go to **Finish**. Reboot the Raspberry Pi. Now, you can go ahead and start using your camera module.

Usage of modules

In this section, you will learn how to use the module by taking a picture and capturing a video using the Raspberry Pi camera module.

Taking a picture

Create a file `cameraImage.py` with the following script:

```
import picamera
camera = picamera.PiCamera()
camera.capture('image.jpg')
```

The first line makes the `picamera` library available to the script. The second line will create the instance of the `PiCamera` class. The third line will take the picture and store it in the `image.jpg` file.

You have used the Python script to capture an image using the camera module. You can also use the command-line tool that is available to capture an image. `raspistill` is the command-line tool for capturing still images with the camera module. Once you have connected and enabled the camera, run the following command in a terminal to take a picture:

```
raspistill -o cam.jpg
```

The `raspistill` command will take a picture from the camera module, the `-o` flag will store data to the output file and the `cam.jpg` filename, where you want to save the data.

 There are many other options using which you can control the properties of the image taken from a camera module. Some of these options will be discussed in *Chapter 6, Image Processing Algorithms*.

Recording a video

Similar to the previous section, you can use either the command-line tool or can use the Python script to take a video from the camera module. First off, you will take a video using the Python script.

Create a file `cameraVideo.py` with the following script:

```
import picamera
from time import sleep
camera = picamera.PiCamera()
camera.start_recording('video.h264')
sleep(5)
camera.stop_recording()
```

The first two lines make the `picamera` and `time.sleep` libraries available to the script. Line 3 will create the instance of the `PiCamera` class. The fourth line will start recording the video and store it as `video.h264`. The fifth line will wait for 5 seconds using the `sleep` command. The sixth line will stop the recording and the video clip will get saved as `video.h264`.

The `raspivid` is the command-line tool for capturing videos with the camera module. Once you have connected the camera, run the following command in terminal to take a video:

```
raspivid -o video.h264 -t 10000
```

This will record a video for 10 seconds.

The raspivid command will capture a video from the camera module, the -o flag will store the data to the output file and the video.h264 filename where you want to save the data.

If you do not give any -t flag with the length of the video, by default, raspivid will capture a video for 5 seconds.

An Ultrasonic sensor

Ultrasonic sensors work on a principle similar to radar or sonar, which calculates properties of a target by interpreting the echoes from radio or sound waves respectively. This sensor will generate the high frequency sound waves and evaluate the echo, which is received back by the sensor by measuring the time interval between sending the signal and receiving the echo to calculate the distance to an object. In this chapter, you will be using an HC-SR04 ultrasonic sensor Arduino module. It uses sonar to determine the distance to an object. It gives distance with the nearest object with high accuracy and stable reading in an easy-to-use package for distance ranging from 2 cm to 400 cm. Unlike a sharp sensor, which can also be used for measuring the distance, its operation is not affected by sunlight. The following image is an example of ultrasonic sensors:

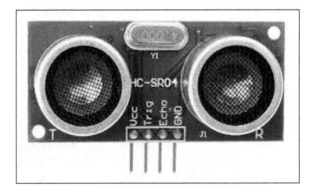

As you can see in the preceding image, there are four pins on HC-SR04:

Vcc: +5VDC

Trig: Trigger input for sensor

Echo: Echo output of the sensor

GND: Ground

First, you need to send the trigger pulse of 10 µs (micro Second) to the **Trig** Pin, which will enable the ultrasonic sensor. The ultrasonic sensor module will send the output to the **Echo** pin.

 The module is not suggested to connect directly to electricity, if connected to electricity, the GND terminal should be connected to the module first; otherwise, it will affect the normal work of the module.

The Raspberry Pi battery

There are many applications where you might want to use Raspberry Pi as a standalone device. The Internet connection and power supply are the only two things that will hinder the use of Raspberry Pi as a standalone device. The Internet connectivity issue can be resolved using the Raspberry Pi WiFi module. To resolve the power supply issue, a rechargeable battery can be used.

The Raspberry Pi Wi-Fi module

As mentioned in the previous section, to make your Raspberry Pi a standalone device, you need to get rid of the Ethernet cable. For this reason, you will be using the Raspberry Pi WiFi module to use the WiFi network. As you know Raspberry Pi doesn't have the capability to connect to the WiFi network, you will be using $5 WiFi module. To make it work, you need to update the current Internet configuration. Here are a few steps that you need to follow to make the WiFi module work properly:

1. Open the terminal and write the following line of code:

   ```
   sudo nano /etc/network/interfaces
   ```

2. You will see something like this in the nano text editor:

   ```
   auto lo
   iface lo inet loopback
   iface eth0 inet dhcp
   ```

   This is a very basic configuration that is used to connect Raspberry Pi to the Internet using an Ethernet cable. You need to modify the interface file to enable the Wi-Fi module. Add the following lines to the interface file:

   ```
   allow-hotplug wlan0
   iface wlan0 inet dhcp
   wpa-conf /etc/wpa_supplicant/wpa_supplicant.conf
   iface default inet dhcp
   ```

Once you have edited the file, press *CTRL + X* to save the file and exit
nano editor.

3. Open the terminal and write this:

```
sudo nano /etc/wpa_supplicant/wpa_supplicant.conf
```

Delete all the content of the file and add the following lines to the file:

```
ctrl_interface=DIR=/var/run/wpa_supplicant GROUP=netdev
update_config=1
network={
ssid="YOURSSID" #It is same as your WiFi network name
psk="YOURPASSWORD" # This is your secret network password

# Protocol type can be: RSN (for WP2) and WPA (for WPA1)
proto=WPA

# Key management type can be: WPA-PSK or WPA-EAP (Pre-
Shared or Enterprise)
key_mgmt=WPA-PSK

# Pairwise can be CCMP or TKIP (for WPA2 or WPA1)
pairwise=TKIP

#Authorization option should be OPEN for both WPA1/WPA2 (in
less commonly used are SHARED and LEAP)
auth_alg=OPEN
}
```

Once you have edited the file , press *CTRL + X* to save and close the file.

4. Now, plug in your WiFi module to the USB port of Raspberry Pi. Updation
   in details such as network configuration are required; you need to reboot to
   apply those changes. Once again, open the terminal and restart Raspberry Pi
   using the following command:

```
sudo reboot
```

5. When the device finishes rebooting, it should automatically connect to the
   WiFi network. Open Midori browser and try accessing the Internet to check
   whether Raspberry Pi is connected to Internet or not.

In this section, you were introduced to a few more electronics components that will
be used in the next section for building the remote-controlled robot.

Developing a remote-controlled robot with live feed and live distance to the nearest wall

Having understood the important electronic components in this section, you will develop a remote controlled robot with live camera feed and live distance to the nearest wall. Similar to the previous chapter, in this chapter, you will develop a couple of small projects and then combine all of them to make a larger project. You can develop three small projects and then merge it to make a larger project:

- Calculating distance using an ultrasonic sensor
- Displaying a live feed from the Raspberry Pi camera module
- Developing a remote-controlled robot using the Raspberry Pi

Calculating distance using an ultrasonic sensor

Before you go ahead make sure you have all the components listed here:

- Raspberry Pi
- Raspberry Pi power supply
- The HC-SR04 ultrasonic sensor
- Hook up wires
- 330 Ohm resistor
- 470 Ohm resistor

 If you don't get a 330 Ohm and 470 Ohm resistor, you can use five 1K Ohm resistors. You can connect three 1K Ohm resistors in parallel instead of a 330 Ohm resistor, and you can connect two 1K Ohm resistor in parallel instead of a 470 Ohm resistor.

Setting up Raspberry Pi

Only Python and the Raspberry Pi GPIO library are required to be installed on Raspberry Pi, which you will install in *Chapter 5, Introduction to Image Processing*, so no additional setup is required.

Connecting ultrasonic sensors pins and Raspberry Pi pins

As mentioned in the ultrasonic sensor introduction section, powering up the module is easy. First, you need to connect the GND pin to the Raspberry Pi GND Pin, that is, Pin 6. Once you have connected the GND pin, connect the Vcc pin to Pin 2 of Raspberry Pi, which can provide 5V DC. The input pin on the module is called the Trig, which is used to trigger the sending of the ultrasonic pulse. Ideally, it wants a 5V pulse, but it works fine with a 3.3 V signal provided from Raspberry Pi GPIO pins. Connect Trig to Pin 24 of the Raspberry Pi. The output pin on the module is called Echo. The output pin remains low (0V) when the module has taken the distance measurement. This sets the Echo pin HIGH (5V) for the amount of time that it took to return the pulse. This module uses +5V as HIGH, but it is too HIGH for Raspberry Pi GPIO as it operates in 3.3 V. If you give +5V to the Raspberry Pi GPIO, it might affect the normal functionality of Raspberry Pi, so to avoid this situation, you can use a level converter, which was introduced in the previous section. However, here you can create a basic voltage divider circuit using two resistors.

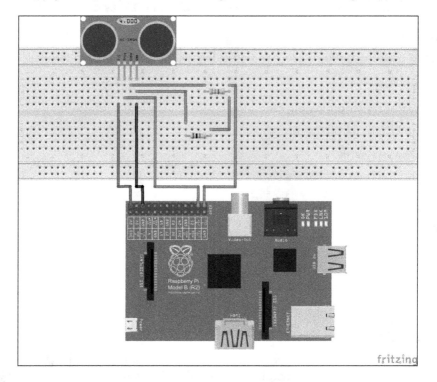

Here is the complete connection diagram. In this circuit, Raspberry Pi Pin 24 and Pin 26 are used for Trigger and Echo respectively. You can use any other GPIO pins of the Raspberry Pi, and you can update the script accordingly.

Scripting

Once you have connected ultrasonic sensor pins with Raspberry Pi as per the diagram, boot up your Raspberry Pi.

Create a new python script by right-clicking on **Create** | **New File** | Ultrasonic.py.

Here is the code that needs to be copied in the file Ultrasonic.py:

```
#Setup Start

import time
import RPi.GPIO as GPIO

GPIO.setmode(GPIO.BCM)

GPIO_TRIGGER = 8
GPIO_ECHO = 7

GPIO.setup(GPIO_TRIGGER,GPIO.OUT)   # Trigger
GPIO.setup(GPIO_ECHO,GPIO.IN)       # Echo

# Set trigger to False (Low)
GPIO.output(GPIO_TRIGGER, False)

# Allow module to settle
time.sleep(0.5)

#SetUp Ends

#Processing Start
# Send 10us pulse to trigger
GPIO.output(GPIO_TRIGGER, True)
time.sleep(0.00001)
GPIO.output(GPIO_TRIGGER, False)

start = time.time()
while GPIO.input(GPIO_ECHO)==0:
  start = time.time()

while GPIO.input(GPIO_ECHO)==1:
  stop = time.time()

# Calculate pulse length
elapsed = stop-start
```

```
distance = elapsed * 34000
distance = distance / 2

print "Ultrasonic Measurement Distance : %.1f" % distance

# Reset GPIO settings
GPIO.cleanup()

#Processing Ends
```

Run the Python script by executing the following line in your terminal:

sudo python Ultrasonic.py

You will see the distance of the nearest wall in centimeters in the output. First step is to get the necessary library:

```
import time
import RPi.GPIO as GPIO
```

It will import the required Python library. In this case, only time and the GPIO library is required.

```
GPIO.setmode(GPIO.BCM)
```

This uses GPIO.BCM references instead of physical pin numbers. Throughout this book, you will be using the BCM.GPIO reference to maintain the consistency.

```
GPIO_TRIGGER = 8
GPIO_ECHO = 7
```

The preceding lines defines the GPIO port number, which will be used for Trigger and Echo. As mentioned earlier, Pin 24 (BCM.GPIO Pin number 8) and Pin 26 (BCM.GPIO Pin number 7) will be used for Trigger and Echo respectively.

```
GPIO.setup(GPIO_TRIGGER,GPIO.OUT)   # Trigger
GPIO.setup(GPIO_ECHO,GPIO.IN)       # Echo
```

This will set up the GPIO port of Raspberry Pi as OUT and IN. It will set the GPIO Trigger pin as OUTPUT as you will be sending the Trigger signal to the ultrasonic module. Similarly, it will set the GPIO Echo pin as INPUT as you will get the response from the ultrasonic module once you have sent the Trigger pulse to the module. To send a trigger, first you need to setup the Trigger pin to FALSE to avoid sending any unwanted pulse:

```
GPIO.output(GPIO_TRIGGER, False)
    time.sleep(0.5)
```

It will set Trigger to `False` (Low), and after this, it will wait for `0.5` seconds, which will give enough time to the module to settle.

```
GPIO.output(GPIO_TRIGGER, True)
time.sleep(0.00001)
GPIO.output(GPIO_TRIGGER, False)
```

As mentioned in the ultrasonic sensor module section, first you need to send the 10 µs Trigger pulse to the `Trigger` pin, and then the module will send the output to the `Echo` pin. Next step is to measure the time that is taken by sound waves to bounce back:

```
start = time.time()
while GPIO.input(GPIO_ECHO)==0:
  start = time.time()

while GPIO.input(GPIO_ECHO)==1:
  stop = time.time()
```

Once you have sent the Trigger pulse, as explained in the ultrasonic sensor module section, after some time, you will receive the reflected sound waves. You need to calculate the time that is taken by sound waves to bounce back.

```
elapsed = stop-start
distance = elapsed * 34000
distance = distance / 2
```

Calculate the pulse length by finding the time difference between `start` and `stop`. The distance pulse travelled in that time is time multiplied by the speed of sound (cm/s), that is, `34000` cm/s. This is the total distance that is covered by the sound waves. To calculate the `distance` to the nearest wall, you need to divide it by `2`.

```
print "Ultrasonic Measurement Distance : %.1f" % distance
GPIO.cleanup()
```

It will print the distance on the screen, and after this, it will reset the GPIO pin settings.

Displaying live feed from the Raspberry Pi camera module

In this section, you will develop a project in which you can see the live feed from the camera module in the browser. Before you start working on this project, make sure you have the following components with you:

- Raspberry Pi
- The Raspberry Pi camera module
- Internet connectivity on Raspberry Pi

Setting up Raspberry Pi

In this project, you will live stream from the Raspberry Pi camera, and for live streaming, you will need a web server installed on your Raspberry Pi. For this, you will be using Apache web server with PHP support. For live streaming of the video from the Raspberry Pi camera module, you will use the MJPG-streamer library. Before you start using MJPEG-library, there is a dependency library that needs to be installed. In your terminal, execute this to install the dependency library and Apache server with PHP support:

```
sudo apt-get install libv4l-dev libjpeg8-dev subversion
imagemagick libapache2-mod-php5 php5 apache2
```

Once you have all the dependency installed, check out the MJPEG-streamer repo by typing the following command in terminal:

```
svn co https://svn.code.sf.net/p/mjpg-streamer/code/ MJPG-streamer
```

Once this gets completed, you will get the MJPEG-streamer folder. You have checked out the MJPEG-streamer source files to your Raspberry Pi. Now, you need to build it so that you can use it. Run the following command in your terminal to create the necessary executables:

```
cd MJPG-streamer/mjpg-streamer
```

```
sudo make USE_LIBV4L2=true
```

This will generate some executable and shared libraries in this folder. This folder should contain the following files:

- mjpg_streamer (binary)
- input_uvc.so
- input_file.so
- output_http.so

Cross-check by opening the MJPG-streamer/mjpg-streamer folder.

Connecting the Raspberry Pi and Raspberry Pi camera module

The Raspberry Pi camera module can be used to take full HD 1080p photos as well as video. This can also be controlled programmatically. You already saw a couple of examples in *The Raspberry Pi camera* section. The camera may come with a small piece of translucent blue plastic film covering the lens. It is there just to protect the lens while it is getting shipped to you. Once you have received it, you may remove it by gently peeling it off.

The camera module that you bought has also come with the flex cable. This flex cable should be connected to the connector S5 situated between the Ethernet and HDMI ports. This connector should be opened by pulling the tabs on top of the connector, upwards then towards the Ethernet port. The flex cable should be inserted firmly into the connector, with care taken not to bend the flex at too acute an angle. The top part of the connector should then be pushed towards the HDMI connector and down, while the flex cable is held in place.

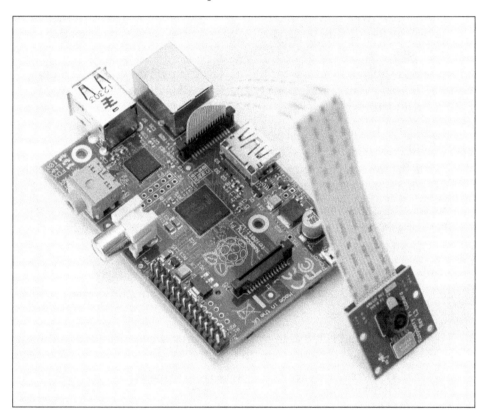

Scripting

The streaming server needs a sequence of JPEG files to stream, and for this, you will use the `raspistill` utility that is part of Raspbian to which you are already familiar with. The `raspistill` utility uses the JPEG encoder, which will run in the GPU, so the load required to generate the JPEG is much less and it does not have a major effect on the performance of Raspberry Pi:

1. First, you need to create a directory where the JPEG stream will get created. Run the following command in the terminal window:

   ```
   mkdir /home/pi/stream
   ```

2. Once you have created the directory, run the following command in the terminal to create a continuous stream of images:

```
raspistill -w 640 -h 480 -q 5 -o /home/pi/stream/pic.jpg -tl 100
-t 9999999 -th 0:0:0 -n &
```

-w sets the image width. For an HD stream use 1920 here.

-h sets the image height. For an HD stream use 1080 here.

-q sets the JPEG quality level, from 0 to 100. Here it is a pretty low quality that is 5, better quality generates bigger pictures, which reduces the frame rate.

-o sets the output filename for the JPEG pictures. You will send them to a /home/pi/stream directory. The same file will be rewritten with updated pictures.

-tl sets the timelapse interval, in milliseconds. With a value of 100 you get 10 frames per second.

-t sets the time the program will run. You need to put a large number here, that amounts to about two hours of run time.

-th sets the thumbnail picture options. Since I want the pictures to be as small as possible I disabled the thumbnails by setting everything to zero.

-n, Do not display a preview window

& puts the application to run in the background.

So now you have the background task, that is, writing JPEG from camera at a rate of 10 per second.

3. The only thing that is left is to start a streaming server. Run the following command in your command line to start the streaming server:

```
LD_LIBRARY_PATH=/home/pi/MJPG-streamer/mjpg-streamer/
/home/pi/MJPG-streamer/mjpg-streamer/mjpg_streamer -i
"/home/pi/MJPG-streamer/mjpg-streamer/input_file.so -f
/home/pi/stream -n pic.jpg" -o "/home/pi/MJPG-
streamer/mjpg-streamer/output_http.so -p 8081 -w
/home/pi/MJPG-streamer/mjpg-streamer/www" &
```

LD_LIBRARY_PATH sets the path for dynamic link libraries to the current directory. This is so that the application can find the plugins, which are in the same directory.

-isets the input plugin. You need to use a plugin called input_file.so. This plugin watches a directory and any time it detects a JPEG file was written to it it streams that file.

-f sets the folder to watch for MJPEG stream

-o sets the output plugin. You will use the HTTP streaming plugin, which starts a web server that you can connect to to watch the video.

-p sets the port number on which you can watch the video

-w sets the root directory of the web server. You will use the default web pages that come with the application for now, these can be changed and customized as necessary.

& puts the application to run in the background.

4. Now, you have everything ready. You can check the live stream from the Raspberry Pi camera module on any device that has a web browser and is connected to the same network as Raspberry Pi. Open the browser and connect to the following website:

    ```
    http://<IP-ADDRESS>:8081
    ```

    Here, IP-ADDRESS is the IP address of the Raspberry Pi where the web server is hosted.

    The default website served by the streaming server provides access to several players to watch the stream. Go to the **Stream** section, where you will be able to see the live stream. For now, you can use this default page, but in the later part of this chapter, you will create an HTML/PHP page where you can include this stream.

Developing a remote-controlled robot using Raspberry Pi

In this section, you will develop a remote-controlled robot. Before you get started, make sure you have the following components with you:

*   Raspberry Pi
*   4 wheels
*   4 DC motors of 200 RPM
*   Hook-Up wires
*   Robotic base
*   L293D motor driver IC
*   Power bank (Todo: Add the details of power bank that you have used)

Setting up Raspberry Pi

Python and Raspberry Pi GPIO libraries are required to be installed on Raspberry Pi, which you have already installed in *Chapter 5, Introduction to Image Processing*. For controlling the robot remotely, you need to install the web server on the Raspberry Pi, which you already did in the previous section.

Connecting Raspberry Pi pins and robot

Once you have all the component handy with you, and after you have set up the Raspberry Pi, you will require motor driver IC L293D to control the motors. First, you need to connect the motors to the robotic base. Once this is done, you can connect the Raspberry Pi and motor driver IC and DC motors; as per the following diagram you can do the connection in two steps. First, connect the motors with the motor driver IC, and then connect the motor driver IC with Raspberry Pi GPIO pins.

As mentioned earlier in the section of *Motor driver IC*, a single L293D can simultaneously control two motors. In the current case, where you are using four DC motors, you will require to have two L293D IC; however, for simplicity in the following diagram, two motors are connected in parallel to each side of the single L293D IC.

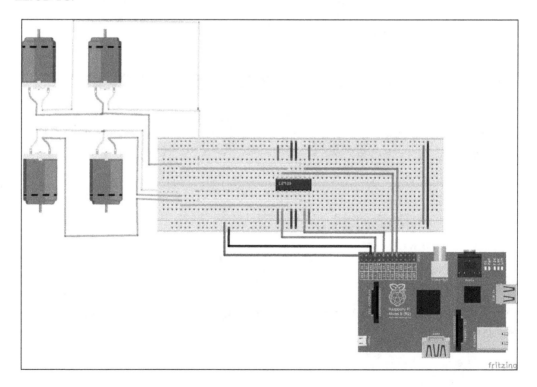

Scripting

Once you have connected the Raspberry Pi pins with the L293D pins, you can start scripting for controlling the GPIO ports of Raspberry Pi using the web server. For this, you need to add www-data to sudoers because for accessing GPIO ports of the Raspberry Pi, you require sudo (super user) permissions:

```
sudo echo "www-data ALL=(ALL) NOPASSWD: ALL" >> /etc/sudoers
```

The preceding command will add www-data (the web server files) to the sudo user group, which can access the GPIO ports of the Raspberry Pi without any password.

To control the Raspberry Pi GPIO remotely, you will need a user interface, which the user can use to send the command to the web server, and then the web server will send the command to control the GPIO of the Raspberry Pi.

Creating a user interface for controlling the robot

1. Execute the following command in your terminal to create a folder specific to this project:

   ```
   mkdir /home/pi/remoteRobot
   ```

2. Close the terminal and create a new file by right-clicking on **Create** | **File** | remoteRobot.html. Paste the following code in the file:

   ```html
   <html>
   <head>
   <meta http-equiv="Content-Type" content="text/html;
   charset=UTF-8">
   <title>Raspberry Pi remote Controlled  Robot</title>
   </head>
   <body>
   <center>
     <div id="controls">
       <a href="remoteRobot.php?GO=ON">Connect to
       Engine</a><br/>
       <img src="controller.png" usemap="#controls" /><br />
     </div>
   <map name="controls">
     <area shape="rect"
     coords="30,1,120,60"href="remoteRobot.php?GO=FORWARD"
     alt="Forward" title="Forward">
     <area shape="rect"
     coords="1,60,70,120"href="remoteRobot.php?GO=LEFT"
     alt="Left" title="Left">
   ```

```
   <area shape="rect"
   coords="30,130,120,180"href="remoteRobot.php?GO=BACKWARD"
   alt="Backward" title="Backward">
   <area shape="rect"
   coords="130,60,180,120"href="remoteRobot.php?GO=RIGHT"
   alt="Right" title="Right">
</map>
</center>
</body>
</html>
```

You have already learned HTML and related concepts in *Chapter 2,
Developing Web Applications*. In the user interface, you will require **START**,
FORWARD, **BACKWARD**, **LEFT**, and **RIGHT** functionality/controls.
Line 1 to Line 7 should be self-explanatory. Line 9 to Line 12 defines the
controls. Initially, for connecting the Robot, Line 10 will create an hyperlink
with remoteRobot.php?GO=ON as the hyperlink reference. You will create
a remoteRobot.php file in the next subsection, which will control the
GPIO of the Raspberry Pi based on the command received from the user
interface page. Line 11 defines the image for other four controls **FORWARD**,
BACKWARD, **LEFT**, and **RIGHT**. Now, to attach events to different parts
of the image, a map is used. The usemap attribute specifies an image as a
client-side image-map (an image-map is an image with clickable areas). The
usemap attribute is associated with a <map> element's name or ID attribute,
and creates a relationship between the <img> and <map> tags. Line 13 to Line
18 maps the area of an image to four clickable areas:

```
<area shape="rect"
coords="30,1,120,60"href="remoteRobot.php?GO=FORWARD"
alt="Forward" title="Forward">
coords - Left Margin, Top Margin , Width , Height
href - hyperlink reference
```

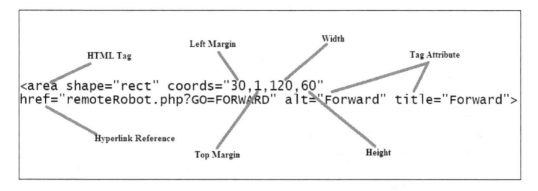

3. The remaining lines of the code should be self-explanatory.

Controlling the movement of the robot

As mentioned in the *Creating a user interface for controlling the robot* section, you need to perform total of five functionalities:

- Initialization
- Forward Movement
- Backward Movement
- Left Movement
- Right Movement

Initialization

You cannot directly access the Raspberry Pi GPIO pins. First, you need to export the GPIO pins that you want to use, and then set it as either out or in based on the requirement. When you want to use the GPIO pin as an output, set it as out. Similarly, if you want to use it as input pin, set it as in. In this section, you will be using 4 GPIO (14,18,24,23) pins and the output of these GPIO pins are used to control the motors, so you need to set all four GPIO ports as out.

Go to the /home/pi/remoteRobot folder and right-click on **Create | New File |** init.sh:

Copy the following code into the file:

```
echo "14" > /sys/class/gpio/export
echo "18" > /sys/class/gpio/export
echo "24" > /sys/class/gpio/export
```

```
echo "23" > /sys/class/gpio/export
echo "out" > /sys/class/gpio/gpio14/direction
echo "out" > /sys/class/gpio/gpio18/direction
echo "out" > /sys/class/gpio/gpio23/direction
echo "out" > /sys/class/gpio/gpio24/direction
```

Robot movement

As per the connection diagram in the *Connecting Raspberry Pi pins and robot* section, it is clear that you need to set GPIO 14 and GPIO 24 to HIGH for FORWARD movement of the robot. Here is the complete table depicting all the movements and related GPIO pins value:

	GPIO 14	GPIO 18	GPIO 24	GPIO 23
Forward	HIGH	LOW	HIGH	LOW
Backward	LOW	HIGH	LOW	HIGH
Left	LOW	HIGH	HIGH	LOW
Right	HIGH	LOW	LOW	HIGH

Forward

Go to the /home/pi/remoteRobot folder and right click on **Create | New File |** forward.sh.

Copy the following code into the file:

```
echo "1" > /sys/class/gpio/gpio14/value
echo "0" > /sys/class/gpio/gpio18/value
echo "1" > /sys/class/gpio/gpio24/value
echo "0" > /sys/class/gpio/gpio23/value
sleep 1
echo "0" > /sys/class/gpio/gpio14/value
echo "0" > /sys/class/gpio/gpio18/value
echo "0" > /sys/class/gpio/gpio24/value
echo "0" > /sys/class/gpio/gpio23/value
```

The first four lines set the GPIO pins as per the preceding table are for the forward movement. After 1 second (sleep 1), all four GPIO pins should be set to LOW; otherwise, the robot will keep on moving in the forward direction.

 In the preceding code, after 1 milliseconds, GPIO pins are set to LOW, so the robot will take some small steps. However, if you want more movement, you may want to increase the time.

Others

Similar to forward movement, all three movements can be configured. Here is the code for the remaining three files:

Go to /home/pi/remoteRobot folder and right-click on **Create | New File |** backward.sh.

Copy the following code into the file:

```
echo "0" > /sys/class/gpio/gpio14/value
echo "1" > /sys/class/gpio/gpio18/value
echo "0" > /sys/class/gpio/gpio24/value
echo "1" > /sys/class/gpio/gpio23/value
sleep 1
echo "0" > /sys/class/gpio/gpio14/value
echo "0" > /sys/class/gpio/gpio18/value
echo "0" > /sys/class/gpio/gpio24/value
echo "0" > /sys/class/gpio/gpio23/value
```

Go to the /home/pi/remoteRobot folder and right-click on **Create | New File |** left.sh.

Copy the following code into the file:

```
echo "0" > /sys/class/gpio/gpio14/value
echo "1" > /sys/class/gpio/gpio18/value
echo "1" > /sys/class/gpio/gpio24/value
echo "0" > /sys/class/gpio/gpio23/value
sleep 1
echo "0" > /sys/class/gpio/gpio14/value
echo "0" > /sys/class/gpio/gpio18/value
echo "0" > /sys/class/gpio/gpio24/value
echo "0" > /sys/class/gpio/gpio23/value
```

Go to the /home/pi/remoteRobot folder and right-click on **Create | New File |** right.sh.

Copy the following code into the file:

```
echo "1" > /sys/class/gpio/gpio14/value
echo "0" > /sys/class/gpio/gpio18/value
echo "0" > /sys/class/gpio/gpio24/value
echo "1" > /sys/class/gpio/gpio23/value
sleep 1
echo "0" > /sys/class/gpio/gpio14/value
echo "0" > /sys/class/gpio/gpio18/value
```

```
echo "0" > /sys/class/gpio/gpio24/value
echo "0" > /sys/class/gpio/gpio23/value
```

Now, you need to move this control script to the webserver folder as you want to control GPIO from there. Open your terminal and execute the following command to copy these files to the /var/www/ folder:

```
cd /home/pi/remoteRobot/
sudo cp init.sh forward.sh backward.sh left.sh right.sh /var/www/
```

Server files that can control the Raspberry Pi GPIO

You have already defined commands in the user interface page (remoteRobot.html) that should be sent to the PHP page. Here is the complete list:

Command	Action	Script
On	This connects to the robot or Initialize the robot	init.sh
Forward	Forward movement	forward.sh
Backward	Backward movement	backward.sh
Left	Left Turn	left.sh
Right	Right Turn	right.sh

You have also written a script, which can control the GPIO from webserver folder. Now, what is left is to call the particular script based on the command received from the user interface page. The preceding table contains the mapping of the command and script that needs to be called.

Go to the /home/pi/remoteRobot folder and right-click on **Create | New File | **remoteRobot.php

Copy the following code into the file:

```php
<?php
session_start();
include "remoteRobot.html";
$action = $_GET['GO'];
switch ($action)
{
  case "ON":
    shell_exec('sudo /bin/bash /var/www/init.sh');
    break;
  case "FORWARD":
    shell_exec('sudo /bin/bash /var/www/forward.sh');
```

```
      break;
  case "BACKWARD":
    shell_exec('sudo /bin/bash /var/www/backward.sh');
    break;
  case "LEFT":
    shell_exec('sudo /bin/bash /var/www/left.sh');
    break;
  case "RIGHT":
    shell_exec('sudo /bin/bash /var/www/right.sh');
    break;
}
?>
```

Line 1 will be used to tell the browser that it is a PHP file and needs to be executed on server. Line 2 will start a new session. Line 3 will include the HTML page that you have created before in this section. Line 4 will store the value for the key GO that has been sent to the PHP page by an user interface page. Once you have received the value of the command, based on the value as per the preceding table, you need to call execute a particular shell script. For example, in the case of ON, a command line 8 will execute the init.sh script. shell_exec is the PHP which can be used to run the shell script from the command line.

You have already copied the control script to the /var/www/ folder so that it can be accessed in the server. Now, you need to move the user interface page and the corresponding server page to the /var/www/ folder so that it can be accessed from anywhere in the same network. Open your terminal and execute the following script to move the remoteRobot.html and remoteRobot.php file to the /var/www/ folder:

cd /home/pi/remoteRobot/

sudo cp remoteRobot.html remoteRobot.php /var/www/

Now, you can control your robot from any machine that is connected to the same network using just a browser. Open the browser and type the following command to control your robot:

```
http://<IP-Address>/remoteRobot.php
where IP-Address - IP Address of Raspberry Pi
```

First, you have to click on **Connect the Robot**. Once robot is connected, you can use the button displayed on the screen to control the robot.

Merging everything

You have developed all the three projects. In this section, you will merge everything to make a large project that is a remote-controlled robot with live streaming and live distance measurement. From the development of the three projects, it is clear that you need to extend the *Developing a remote-controlled robot using Raspberry Pi* section. Before moving ahead, make sure you have all the components mentioned in all the three projects.

Connection

Do not disconnect the connection that you have done in the previous section of *Developing a remote-controlled robot using Raspberry Pi*. In addition to this, you have to connect the Raspberry Pi camera module to the CSI connector as mentioned in the *Displaying live feed from the Raspberry Pi camera module* section. Once you have connected the Raspberry Pi camera, connect the ultrasonic sensor as per the connection diagram mentioned in *Calculating distance using an ultrasonic sensor* section. Once you have connected everything, make sure your connection matches with the connection diagram displayed in the following figure:

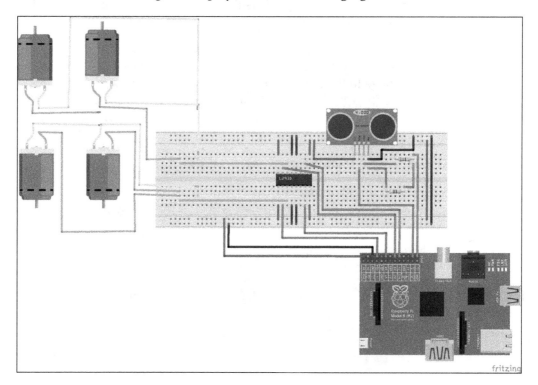

Scripting

From the development of all three projects, it is clear that to merge everything the following files needs to be updated:

- `remoteRobot.html`: User interface needs to be created for displaying live stream as well as live distance measurement.

- `init.sh`: There are some initial commands that need to be executed before you can see the live stream. These commands needs to be included in this file

- `/var/www/`: Copy `ultrasonic.py` file to this folder so that it can be. executed from the web server

Updating the user interface

You need to display the live stream and live ultrasonic measurement distance, for this create two `<div>` tags as follows:

```
<div id="streamdata" style="float: left;">
<img src="http://<IP-address>:8081/?action=stream"/>
</div>
```

The preceding code will display live stream in an image. The image source has been given as `http://<IP-address>:8081/?action=stream`, which is used to get the live stream from the port number `8081`. Next step is to create placeholder where distance measured by ultrasonic sensor will get displayed:

```
<div id="distance">Ultrasonic Measurement Distance
</div>
```

In the previous code, **Ultrasonic Measurement Distance** will get displayed, but currently the script that you have run for a single time does not provide live data. For this, you need to create a script, which will automatically call the ultrasonic python script every one second:

```
<script type="text/javascript">
setInterval(function(){
if(XMLHttpRequest) var x = new XMLHttpRequest();
elsevar x = new ActiveXObject("Microsoft.XMLHTTP");
x.open("GET", "ultrasonic.php", true);
x.send();
x.onreadystatechange = function(){
if(x.readyState == 4){
if(x.status == 200) document.getElementById("distance").innerHTML
= x.responseText;
else document.getElementById("distance").innerHTML = "Error
loading document";
```

```
        }
      }
   },5000);
   </script>
```

You can call the PHP file from the HTML file by making a GET request by assuming you already know what the GET request is. Line 1 will tell the browser that the script that is written inside the <script> tag is JavaScript. setInterval will execute a particular function after every x seconds. In the preceding code, x is 5000, that is 5 seconds. Lines 3 and 4 will create an object HTTP request. XMLHttpRequest and ActiveXObject—because one of these might not work on some browsers. Line 5 will generate an asynchronous (as the third parameter is true) GET(first parameter) request to URL ultrasonic.php. Line 6 will send the GET request to the server and continue other operation as it is asynchronous request. If the state of the request is 4 (Line 8) and status is 200 (Line 9) then Line 10 will display the response on the "distance" <div> placeholder. If the response received is not proper, it will show the error message in "distance" <div> (Line 11)

readyState values

0: Request not initialized

1: Server connection established

2: Request received

3: Processing request

4: Request finished and response is ready

Update the remoteRobot file, which will look like:

```
<html>
<head>
<meta http-equiv="Content-Type" content="text/html; charset=UTF-
8">
<title>Raspberry Pi remote controllled  Robot</title>
</head>
<script type="text/javascript">
setInterval(function(){
if(XMLHttpRequest) var x = new XMLHttpRequest();
elsevar x = new ActiveXObject("Microsoft.XMLHTTP");
x.open("GET", "ultrasonic.php", true);
x.send();
x.onreadystatechange = function(){
if(x.readyState == 4){
if(x.status == 200) document.getElementById("distance").innerHTML
= x.responseText;
```

```
else document.getElementById("distance").innerHTML = "Error
loading document";
        }
    }
},5000);
</script>

<body>

<div>
  <div id="streamdata" style="float: left;">
<img src="http://<IP-address>:8081/?action=stream"/>
  </div>
  <center>
  <div id="controls">
    <a href="remotRobot.php?GO=ON">Connect to Engine</a><br/>
    <img src="controller.png" usemap="#controls" />
    <br /><br/>
  </div>
  <div id="distance">Ultrasonic Measurement Distance
  </div>
  </center>
</div>
<map name="controls">
  <area shape="rect" coords="30,1,120,60"
    href="remoteRobot.php?GO=FORWARD" alt="Forward"
    title="Forward">
  <area shape="rect" coords="1,60,70,120"
    href="remoteRobot.php?GO=LEFT" alt="Left" title="Left">
  <area shape="rect" coords="30,130,120,180"
    href="remoteRobot.php?GO=BACKWARD" alt="Backward"
    title="Backward">
  <area shape="rect" coords="130,60,180,120"
    href="remoteRobot.php?GO=RIGHT" alt="Right" title="Right">
</map>
</body>
</html>
```

Updating server-related files

In the previous section, you have updated the user interface and you wrote
a script that calls the `utrasonic.php` file at every 5 seconds. However, currently,
the `ultrasonic.php` file does not exist. So go to `/home/pi/remoteRobot` folder
and right-click on **Create** | **New File** | `ultrasonic.php`.

Copy the following code in the `ultrasonic.php` file:

```php
<?php
echo shell_exec('sudo python /var/www/ultrasonic.py');
?>
```

It will call the python script every time and `echo` (send the response back), the output provided by the script as a response to the request. You need to move this file as well, `ultrasonic.py`, which you have created in *Calculating distance using an ultrasonic sensor* to the `/var/www/` folder so that you can access it from the web server. Open your terminal and execute the following command to copy it to the `/var/www/` folder:

cd /home/pi/remoteRobot

sudo cp ultrasonic.php ultrasonic.py /var/www/

When you click on **Connect to Robot**, the live stream should get displayed on the screen. For this, you need to modify the `init.sh` file. Add the following lines to the `init.sh` file:

```
raspistill -w 640 -h 480 -q 5 -o /home/pi/stream/pic.jpg -tl 100 -
t 9999999 -th 0:0:0 -n &
LD_LIBRARY_PATH=/home/pi/MJPG-streamer/mjpg-streamer/
/home/pi/MJPG-streamer/mjpg-streamer/mjpg_streamer -i
"/home/pi/MJPG-streamer/mjpg-streamer/input_file.so -f
/home/pi/stream -n pic.jpg" -o "/home/pi/MJPG-streamer/mjpg-
streamer/output_http.so -p 8081 -w /home/pi/MJPG-streamer/mjpg-
streamer/www" &
```

The updated `init.sh` file will look like:

```
raspistill -w 640 -h 480 -q 5 -o /home/pi/stream/pic.jpg -tl 100 -
t 9999999 -th 0:0:0 -n &
LD_LIBRARY_PATH=/home/pi/MJPG-streamer/mjpg-streamer/
/home/pi/MJPG-streamer/mjpg-streamer/mjpg_streamer -i
"/home/pi/MJPG-streamer/mjpg-streamer/input_file.so -f
/home/pi/stream -n pic.jpg" -o "/home/pi/MJPG-streamer/mjpg-
streamer/output_http.so -p 8081 -w /home/pi/MJPG-streamer/mjpg-
streamer/www" &
echo "14" > /sys/class/gpio/export
echo "18" > /sys/class/gpio/export
echo "24" > /sys/class/gpio/export
echo "23" > /sys/class/gpio/export
echo "out" > /sys/class/gpio/gpio14/direction
echo "out" > /sys/class/gpio/gpio18/direction
echo "out" > /sys/class/gpio/gpio23/direction
echo "out" > /sys/class/gpio/gpio24/direction
```

That's it! Now, you have merged all the three projects. Open a browser from a device from which you want to control the robot and open the following URL:

```
http://<IP-address>/remoteRobot.php
```

Here, IP-address is the IP address of the Raspberry Pi:

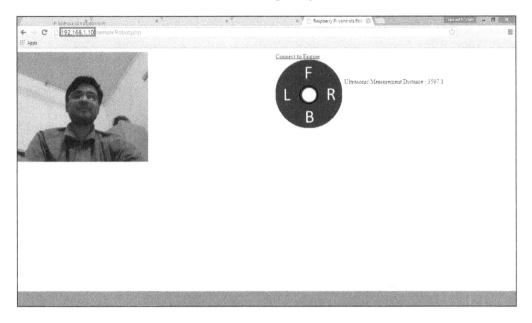

If you click on **Connect to Robot**, you will be able to see the live stream from the camera module on the screen. At the same time, just below the controller image, you will also be able to see the distance to the nearest wall in centimeters. This will automatically get updated after every 5 seconds.

Summary

In this chapter, a few more electronics components were introduced, which were used in the later part of the chapter to develop a remote-controlled robot, which can also live stream video data as well as display real-time distance to the nearest wall.

In the next chapter, an area of image processing will be introduced. The basic concept of image processing will be introduced in the first few section of the chapter. In the later part of the chapter, using image processing library a time-lapse video camera and Twitter-controlled Raspberry Pi camera module will be developed.

5

Introduction to Image Processing

In today's modern science and technology areas, images and videos have gained broader scope due to the ever-growing importance of scientific visualization and digitization. In this chapter, you will get introduced to the basics of image processing. Once you have understood the basics of image processing, the image processing library, which needs to be installed on Raspberry Pi, will get introduced. Later in this chapter, we will perform basic image processing operation on Raspberry Pi followed by interesting projects creating a time-lapse video and Twitter-controlled Raspberry Pi camera. The following topics are covered in this chapter:

- What is image processing?
- The Raspberry Pi camera module
- A image processing library
- A quick start to image processing
- Creating a time-lapse video with a Raspberry Pi camera
- Developing a Twitter-controlled Raspberry Pi camera

What is image processing?

Of the five human senses—vision, hearing, smell, taste, and touch—vision is undoubtedly the major source of input/information to the human brain. Human eyes provide information in a range of megabits per glance. However, much of this information is redundant and several layers of visual cortex compress this information so that higher centers of the brain have to interpret only a small fraction of the input data. The ultimate goal of areas such as computer vision is to use a computer to emulate human vision, including learning and being able to take actions based on visual inputs. A computer vision can be defined as the process of deciphering the physical contents of an image/video by computer/machine. This chapter will focus on a high-level image processing, which is often referred to as computer vision.

 Some authors refer to computer vision as machine vision.

A computer vision is a rapidly growing field, partly as a result of both cheaper and more capable cameras, partly because of an affordable processing power, and partly because vision algorithms are starting to mature.

Today, for most of the software professionals and students, image processing has become anonymous to digital image processing in which the input is an image and the output is a processed image, which may be either modified image as per the user's requirements or parameters related to the image. So, in simple terms, image processing is a process of getting useful information from the supplied input image by analyzing/modifying the image.

 A detailed study of image processing is out of the scope of this book.

Images and types of images

A digital image can be considered as a discrete representation of data possessing both spatial (layout) and intensity (color) information. When trying to recreate the physical world in a digital format via a camera, for example, the computer just sees the image in the form of a code that just contains the numbers 1 and 0. A digital image is nothing but a collection of pixels (picture elements), which are then stored in matrices or any other suitable format that will be understood by image processing library for further manipulation. In the matrices, each element contains information about a particular pixel in the image. The pixel value decides how bright or what color that pixel should be. Based on this, images can be classified images:

- Grayscale
- Color/RGB

 Pixels are the smallest constituent elements in a digital image and contain a numerical value, which is the basic unit of information within the image.

The grayscale image

In the grayscale image, the pixel value can range from 0 to 255 where 0 being black and 255 being white. As pixels in the grayscale image can vary from 0 to 255, several shades of gray color are visible in the following image:

 You might be wondering why 0 to 255 and why not other numbers. This is because as a starting point I have taken the example of 8-bit images. 8-bit means 2^8=256. So, here the value will vary from 0 to 255.

A special case of a grayscale image is the binary image or the black and white image where each pixel of an image can have a value of either 0 or 255. Here is a black and white image:

Color/RGB

As you know, red, blue, and green are the fundamental/primary colors. Different colors can be made by different proportion of red, green, and blue. For each channel, the pixel value can be in the range of 0 to 255. Here's the color image:

Image formats

From a mathematical viewpoint, any meaningful 2-D array of numbers can be considered as an image. In the real world, we need to effectively display images, store them (preferably compactly), transmit them over networks, and recognize bodies of numerical data as corresponding to images. This has led to the development of standard digital image formats. In simple terms, the image formats comprise a file header (containing information on how exactly the image data is stored) and the actual numeric pixel values themselves. There are many image formats available today. However, the most widely used image formats are shown in the following table:

Acronym	Name	Properties
GIF	Graphics Interchange Format	This is limited to only 256 colors (8-bit), lossless compression
JPEG	Joint Photographic Expert Group	This is most widely used today; lossy compression
BMP	Bit Map Picture	This is a basic image format; lossless compression
PNG	Portable Network Graphics	This is a new lossless compression format
TIF/TIFF	Tagged Image Format (File)	This is a highly flexible, detailed and adaptable format

As suggested in the Properties column of the preceding table, different image formats are suitable for different applications. Basically, different image formats came into existence because raw images (as mentioned in the previous section of Grayscale and RGB image) require more space on your machine.

Applications of image processing

The history of image processing is intimately tied to the development of the digital computer. The first computers powerful enough to carry out meaningful image processing tasks appeared in the early 1960s. The work on using computer techniques to improve images from a space probe began at the Jet Propulsion Laboratory (Pasadena, California) in 1964 when pictures of the moon transmitted by Ranger 7 were processed by a computer to correct various types of image distortion in the on-board television camera. In parallel with space applications, digital image processing techniques began in the late 1960s and early 1970s to be used in medical imaging, remote Earth resources observations, and astronomy. Today, there is almost no area of technical endeavor that is not impacted in some way by digital image processing.

As mentioned earlier, the focus of this chapter is on computer vision/machine vision. Here are the typical problems in the machine vision that utilize image processing: automatic character recognition, industrial machine vision for product assembly and inspection, military recognizance, automatic processing of fingerprints, screening of X-rays and blood samples, and machine processing of aerial and satellite imagery for weather prediction and environmental assessment. In this chapter and the next chapter, you will learn about some of the image processing techniques used in the preceding applications. However, to give you a feel of how important the image processing field has become today, here are some image processing applications categorized according to the image source:

 Here the image sources are categorized based on the electromagnetic spectrum: gamma rays, X-rays, ultraviolet, visible, infrared, microwaves, and radio waves.

Image source	Applications
Gamma rays	Nuclear medicine
	Astronomical observation
X-rays	Medical diagnostics (angiography and **computerized axial tomography** (CAT)scan)
	Astronomy
Ultraviolet	Lithography
	Industrial inspection
	Microscopy
	Lasers
	Biological imaging
	Astronomical observations
Visible and infrared	Visual imaging
	Microscopy
	Astronomy
	Remote sensing
	Law enforcement
Microwave	Radar
Radio wave	Medicine, **magnetic resonance imaging (MRI)**
	Astronomy

The Raspberry Pi camera module

You were introduced to the Raspberry Pi camera module in *Chapter 4*, *Getting into Robotics*. It can be used to take high-definition video as well as still photographs. This can be attached via a 15 cm ribbon cable to the CSI port on Raspberry Pi. It's easy to use for beginners, but has plenty to offer (such as time-lapse, slow-motion, and other video cleverness) for advanced users. The camera module is very popular in home security applications and in wildlife camera traps. Now, you have some knowledge about image and pixel. Here are more details of the Raspberry Pi camera module:

- Sensor resolution: 2592 * 1944 Pixels

- Pixel size: 1.4um * 1.4 um

- Picture formats: JPEG (accelerated), JPEG + RAW, GIF, BMP, PNG, YUV420, RGB888

- Video format: raw h.264 (accelerated)

The image processing library

In the previous section, you understood about image processing and its applications. To develop your image processing algorithms, you require some infrastructure/library or you would end up doing everything from scratch by yourself. In this book, we will use the OpenCV library for writing/developing image processing algorithms. OpenCV stands for open source computer vision. It has played a role in the growth of computer vision by enabling thousands of people to do more productive work in vision. With its focus on real-time vision, OpenCV helps students and professionals efficiently implement projects and jump-start research by providing them with a computer vision and machine learning infrastructure that was previously available only in a few mature research labs.

Introduction to OpenCV

OpenCV is the world's most popular open source computer vision library, which contains over 500 functions that span many areas in vision as well as robotics. The library is written in C and C++ and it runs under all three major platforms, that is, Linux, Windows, and Mac OS X. It was designed for computational efficiency and with a strong focus on real-time applications. Today, whenever you talk about computer vision, machine learning will come into play some or the other way and vice versa. Because of the same reason, OpenCV contains a full, general purpose **Machine Learning Library (MLL)**.

Machine learning is an area of computer science that deals with the construction and study of algorithms that can be learned from data.

OpenCV is broadly structured into five main components that are mentioned in the following table:

Component Name	Capabilities
CV	Image processing and higher-level computer vision algorithms
MLL	Machine Learning Library contains many statistical classifiers and clustering tools
HighGUI	GUI, Image, and Video I/O
CXCORE	Basic structures and algorithms, XML support, and drawing functions
CvAux	Background-foreground segmentation, Eigen objects, and Stereovision

Although the preceding table explained the core components of OpenCV, researchers and scientists who extensively use OpenCV talk in the language of OpenCV modules. The following table contains a brief description of important modules:

Module	Feature
Core	This is a compact module defining basic data structures, including the dense multidimensional array, Mat, and the basic functions used by all other modules
Imgproc	This is an image processing module that includes linear and nonlinear image filtering, geometrical image transformations (resizing, affine and perspective warping, and generic table-based remapping), color space conversion, histograms, and so on
Video	This is a video analysis module that includes motion estimation, background subtraction, and object tracking algorithms
Calib3d	This consists of basic multiple-view geometry algorithms, single and stereo camera calibration, object pose estimation, stereo correspondence algorithms, and elements of 3D reconstruction
Features2d	This consists of salient feature detectors, descriptors, and descriptor matchers
Objdetect	The features include detection of objects and instances of the predefined classes; for example, faces, eyes, mugs, people, and cars
Highgui	This is an easy-to-use interface for video capturing, image and video codecs as well as simple UI capabilities
GPU	The features of GPU include GPU-accelerated algorithms from different OpenCV modules

OpenCV is distributed with a BSD license, which means that you can make a commercial application without revealing your source code. However, there are a few algorithms, despite being provided with complete source code inside OpenCV, which are patented.

Installation

This section will cover the installation procedure for Raspbian OS. As Raspbian OS is built on top of the Linux kernel, you will be able to install OpenCV on Raspberry Pi. Newer versions of the OpenCV library are released periodically. For the purpose of this book, the 2.4.1 (the first approach) and 2.4.10 (the second approach) versions have been the reference.

The first approach

If you are not interested in installing the latest version of OpenCV, you can install it from the software repositories by running the following command in the terminal:

```
sudo apt-get update
```

```
sudo apt-get install ipython python-opencv python-scipy python-numpy
python-setuptools python-pip
```

```
sudo apt-get install libopencv-dev
```

```
sudo apt-get update
```

Check the OpenCV version:

```
pkg-config --modversion opencv
```

The second approach

Use this approach if you want the latest/specific version of OpenCV. In this approach, OpenCV will be built from the source and you will have to install the dependencies prior to this:

```
sudo apt-get -y install build-essential cmake cmake-curses-gui pkg-config
libpng12-0 libpng12-dev libpng++-dev libpng3 libpnglite-dev zlib1g-dbg
zlib1g zlib1g-dev pngtools libtiff4-dev libtiff4 libtiffxx0c2 libtiff-
tools libeigen3-dev
```

```
sudo apt-get -y install libjpeg8 libjpeg8-dev libjpeg8-dbg libjpeg-
progs ffmpeg libavcodec-dev libavcodec53 libavformat53 libavformat-dev
libgstreamer0.10-0-dbg libgstreamer0.10-0 libgstreamer0.10-dev libxine1-
ffmpeg libxine-dev libxine1-bin libunicap2 libunicap2-dev swig libv41-0
libv41-dev python-numpy libpython2.6 python-dev python2.6-dev libgtk2.0-
dev
```

Don't worry if you don't understand what these lines mean. Once you have installed the dependencies, download the latest version of OpenCV from `http://opencv.org/downloads.html` (download OpenCV for Linux). Copy the `opencv-2.4.10.zip` to /home/pi directory and run the following commands:

```
unzip opencv-2.4.10.zip
cd opencv-2.4.10
mkdir release
cd release
ccmake ../
```

Press *g* to generate a file. And finally, you need to build the OpenCV library and run the following command:

```
make
sudo make install
```

Please note that this build usually takes more time (around 10 hours) on Raspberry Pi. That's it. OpenCV is now installed on Raspberry Pi.

A quick start to image processing

Once OpenCV is installed on your Raspberry Pi, you can start working on one of the widely used image processing library. In this section, you will learn how to perform basic image operations such as opening an image, reading an image, saving the image to other format and pixel manipulation, and so on. You will also learn about arithmetic operation on images, reading a video file, and opening a video file.

Reading and opening an image

One of the very basic operations in image processing is reading and opening an image.

1. Open your terminal window and create a new folder titled `chapter5` in which you will put all your code by executing the following command:

    ```
    cd /home/pi/
    mkdir chapter5
    ```

2. Create a new python file using this code:

    ```
    nano readImage.py
    ```

3. Copy any of the image file to the chapter5 folder. I had the test.jpg image in the folder. Copy the following command in the file using this code:

```
#import the python opencv module
import cv2
#imread will read an image
img=cv2.imread('/home/pi/chapter5/test.jpg') #Don't forget
to update image name if your image name is different
#show an image in new window titled "image"
cv2.imshow('image' , img)
#press ANY key to close the windows
cv2.waitKey(0)
#close the opened window
cv2.destroyAllWindows()
```

 If you don't use cv2.waitKey(0), a new window will open and close instantaneously. If you do this, Raspberry Pi will wait for your response, and once you press any key, it will close the window.

Saving the image in other formats

In this section, you will convert a JPEG image to the PNG format. You can choose any other image format as well.

Create new python file using this code:

```
nano writeImage.py
```

Copy any of the image file to the `chapter5` folder. I had the `samarth.jpg` image in the folder. Copy the following command in the file:

```
# import python opencv module
import cv2
#imread will read an image
img=cv2.imread('/home/pi/chapter5/samarth.jpg) #Don't forget to
update image name if your image name is different
#show an image in new window titled "image"
cv2.imshow('image',img)
#If you press any key , its ASCII value will get stored in 'key'
variable
key=cv2.waitKey(0)
if key==27
   cv2.destroyAllWindows() #if you press ESC ( ASCII code is 27)
   key , it will close all windows
elif key==ord('s')
   cv2.imwrite('/home/pi/chapter5/samarth.png',img) #if you press
   'S' key , it will save image as PNG
   cv2.destroyAllWindows() # Close all windows
```

In the preceding two examples, you learned about reading and writing images. Here are the two functions used:

```
cv2.imread(IMAGE PATH , IMAGE FLAG)
```

IMAGE PATH: This is the full path of an image that you want to read.

IMAGE FLAG: This specifies the way an image should be read.

- `cv2.imread_COLOR`: This loads a color image. Any transparency of image will be neglected. It is the default flag.

- `cv2. imread_GRAYSCALE`: This loads an image in the grayscale mode.

- `cv2. imread_UNCHANGED`: This loads images as such, including alpha channel.

Alternatively, you can use integers 1, 0, or -1 respectively for the second parameter.

```
cv2.imwrite(IMAGE PATH , IMAGEDATA)
```

IMAGE PATH : This is the full path of an image where you want to write/save an image.

IMAGEDATA : This is the image data that you have got by reading an image.

Saving the image as a grayscale image

In this section, you will save existing color image to a grayscale image:

1. Create a new python file using this code:

    nano writeImage.py

2. Copy the following command in the file:

    ```
    # import python opencv module
    import cv2
    #imread will read an image
    img=cv2.imread('/home/pi/chapter5/samarth.jpg,0) #Read Image as
    grayscale image
    #show an image in new window titled "image"
    cv2.imshow('image',img)
    #If you press any key , its ASCII value will get stored in 'key'
    variable
    key=cv2.waitKey(0)
    if key==27
      cv2.destroyAllWindows() #if you press ESC ( ASCII code is 27)
      key , it will close all windows
    elif key==ord('s')
      cv2.imwrite('/home/pi/chapter5/Samarth_grayscale.jpg',img) #if
      you press 'S' key , it will save image
      cv2.destroyAllWindows() # Close all windows
    ```

You already know how to take a picture from the Raspberry Pi camera, so I haven't included it in this section. Refer to *Chapter 4, Getting into Robotics, The Raspberry Pi camera* section.

Pixel-related operation on the image

You learned about basic image operation in the last section. Image processing researches work with individual pixels of an image most of the time. In this section, you will learn how you can access individual pixels of an image using a Python interactive shell (IPython) as pixel-related operations are often required, and you might not want to create a different project for obtaining minor information.

> You can open the IPython interactive shell by typing `ipython` in the Raspberry Pi terminal.

Accessing and modifying pixel values

First, you need to read the image before reading its pixel data:

```
import cv2
importnumpy as np # It is numeric python. You will need this for
most of the mathematical operation.
img = cv2.imread('/home/pi/chapter5/samarth.jpg')
```

An individual pixel value can be accessed by its row and column coordinates. For the BGR image, it returns an array of blue, green, and red values. For example, the `[200,200]` pixel value can be read using this code:

```
pixel=img[200,200]
print pixel
[127 200 145]
```

> For a grayscale image, the intensity corresponding to a particular pixel is returned.

Similarly, an individual pixel value can be modified using this code:

```
img[200,200]=[227,227,227]
print img[200,200]
[227,227,227]
```

Accessing image properties

Here are some of the properties that can be accessed using OpenCV:

Operation	Example	Function

Shape of an image	`Print img.shape`
	
	`(948,643,3)`
		This returns a tuple of number of rows, columns, and channels (if the image is color).

Pixels of an image	`Print img.size`
	
	`1828692`
		This returns the total number of pixels of an image.

Split an image	`b,g,r = cv2.split(img)`	This will split an image into individual planes.
Merging an image	`img = cv2.` `merge((b,g,r))`	This will merge all the three planes into a BGR image.
Image datatype	`img.dtype()`	This will return a datatype of the image. `img.dtype` (usually, type=uint8) is very important while debugging because a large number of errors in the OpenCV-Python code are caused by an invalid datatype.

 As I mentioned earlier, Python is an interactive shell. You can see all the properties that OpenCV can get for you by pressing *TAB* twice after `img` in the terminal window.

```
pi@raspberrypi: ~/chapter7                          _ □ x
File  Edit  Tabs  Help

In [2]  img=cv2.imread('/home/pi/chapter7/test.PNG')

In [3]  img.
img.T            img.data         img.nbytes       img.size
img.all          img.diagonal     img.ndim         img.sort
img.any          img.dot          img.newbyteorder img.squeeze
img.argmax       img.dtype        img.nonzero      img.std
img.argmin       img.dump         img.prod         img.strides
img.argsort      img.dumps        img.ptp          img.sum
img.astype       img.fill         img.put          img.swapaxes
img.base         img.flags        img.ravel        img.take
img.byteswap     img.flat         img.real         img.tofile
img.choose       img.flatten      img.repeat       img.tolist
img.clip         img.getfield     img.reshape      img.tostring
img.compress     img.imag         img.resize       img.trace
img.conj         img.item         img.round        img.transpose
img.conjugate    img.itemset      img.searchsorted img.var
img.copy         img.itemsize     img.setasflat    img.view
img.ctypes       img.max          img.setfield
img.cumprod      img.mean         img.setflags
img.cumsum       img.min          img.shape

In [3]  img.
```

Arithmetic operations on the image

In this section, arithmetic operations such as addition and subtraction will be performed on images.

Image addition

You can add two images by the OpenCV function, `cv2.add()`, or simply by the NumPy operation, `result = img1 + img2`. Both images should be of the same depth and type, or the second image can just be a scalar value.

 There is a difference between OpenCV addition and NumPy addition. OpenCV addition is a saturated operation, while NumPy addition is a modulo operation.

Here's an example of image addition:

```
>>> x = np.uint8([230])
>>> y = np.uint8([100])

>>> print cv2.add(x,y) # 230+100 = 330 => 255
[[255]]

>>>print x+y          # 230+100 = 330 % 256 = 74
[74]
```

It will be more visible when you add two images. The OpenCV function will provide a better result. Results for both the methods are displayed in the following images.

The original that is used for an arithmetic operation is as follows:

The original that is used for arithmetic operation is as follows:

The image after applying the OpenCV image addition on the preceding images is as follows:

The image after applying the NumPy image addition on the previous image is as follows:

Image blending

Image blending is also image addition, but different weights are given to images so that it gives a feeling of blending or transparency. Create a new Python file using this command:

nano imageBlending.py

Copy the following code to the file imageBlending.py:

```
import cv2
import numpy

img1 = cv2.imread('/home/pi/chapter5/image1.png')
img2 = cv2.imread('/home/pi/chapter5/image2.png')
img = cv2.addWeighted(img1,0.7,img2,0.3,0)
cv2.imshow('img',img)
cv2.waitKey(0)
cv2.destroyAllWindows()
```

Reading and opening a video

In the previous section, you learned about image-related information. In this section, you will learn a more complex thing that is video. Video is nothing but a sequence of images displayed at particular intervals.

Move to the chapter5 folder in your terminal if you have closed the terminal window:

cd /home/pi/chapter5

Create a new Python file using this command:

nano readVideo.py

Copy the following command in the file readVideo.py:

```
import numpy as np #import numeric python module
import cv2 #import opencv python
cap = cv2.VideoCapture('/home/pi/chapter5/samarth.mp4') #It will read
the video file
while(cap.isOpened()):
  ret, frame = cap.read()
  gray = cv2.cvtColor(frame, cv2.COLOR_BGR2GRAY) #Convert each frame
to   grayscale
  cv2.imshow('frame',gray) #display grayscale image
  if cv2.waitKey(34) & 0xFF == ord('q'): # disaply grayscale image and
wait for 34 millisecond before displaying new image
```

```
break
cap.release() # release the videocapture object
cv2.destroyAllWindows() # close the display window
```

 You already know how to capture a video from the Raspberry Pi camera, so I haven't included it in this section. Refer to *Chapter 4, Getting into Robotics, The Raspberry Pi camera* section.

Till this point, you have learned the basics of image processing. In the next two sections, you will create two interesting use cases of the Raspberry Pi camera:

- Creating time-lapse videos with the Raspberry Pi camera
- Developing a Twitter-enabled Raspberry Pi camera (#TweetCam)

Creating time-lapse videos with the Raspberry Pi camera

Many of you might be already knowing what is time-lapse photography and video. For those who don't know, you may have experienced/seen it many times on television or any other digital media. Time-lapse photography is a photography technique whereby the frequency at which frames are captured is much lower than that used to view the sequence, so when played at normal speed, time appears to move faster. It is considered the opposite of high speed/slow motion photography. Some classic subjects of time-lapse photography include evolution of a construction project, people in the city, and plants growing and flowers opening.

From the definition, it is clear that time lapse photography is a two-step process:

- Taking time-lapse pictures
- Merging images into a video

In *Chapter 4, Getting into Robotics*, you already learned about how to take pictures using the Raspberry Pi camera. The only thing that is left is creating a video using images taken by the Raspberry camera.

Taking time-lapse pictures

In *Chapter 4, Getting into Robotics*, you used raspistill to take pictures using the Raspberry Pi camera. Here, you can use the same approach:

```
raspistill -o myimage_%05d.jpg -tl 30000 -t 600000
```

This script will take a photo every 30 seconds for 10 minutes resulting in a sequence of 20 pictures.

The `%05d` will result in a five-digit number appearing in each filename.

Merging images into a video

Once you have all the images, you need some library/method to combine those images and create a video out of it. The `avconv` command is a useful library that can be used for combining these images. Before you move ahead, you need to install it by executing the following command in your terminal windows:

```
sudo apt-get install libav-tools
```

To construct the video from an image sequence that you have, execute the following command in your terminal window:

```
avconv -r 10 -i myimage_%05d.jpg -r 10 -vcodec libx264 -crf 20 -g
15  timelapse.mp4
```

- `r`: This option tells `avconv` to create a video with a frames per second of 10
- `i`: This option tells `avconv` the path of input images
- `vcode`: This option tells `avconv` which video code to use while creating a video
- `crf`: This option tells `avconv` to aim for a quality level of `20`, which is okay for now. Lower values results in a better quality of video, however at the cost of increase in the file size.
- `g`: This option sets the **group of pictures** (**GOP**) value. The video quality and compression ratio depends on the GOP structure. The GOP structure also affects the distortion sensitivity of the video stream due to packet losses. The recommended GOP should be set to half the frame rate.

The preceding two commands will serve the purpose, however, following the pattern of the chapter, you might want to create it using the Python script. For this, you need to perform the following steps:

Go to the `chapter5` folder on your Raspberry Pi by executing the following command in your terminal:

```
cd chapter5
```

Create a new python file `timeLapseCamera.py` inside that folder by executing the following command:

```
nano timeLaspeCamera.py
```

It will open a nano editor. Copy the following code in timeLapseCamera.py:

```
import os
import time


FRAMES = 1000
FPS_IN = 10
FPS_OUT = 24
WAITTIME = 10
FILMLENGTH = float(FRAMES / FPS_IN)


frameCount = 0
while frameCount< FRAMES:
    imageNumber = str(frameCount).zfill(5)
    os.system("raspistill -o image%s.jpg"%(imageNumber))
    frameCount += 1
    time.sleep(WAITTIME - 6) #Takes roughly 6 seconds to take a picture

os.system("avconv -r %s -i image%s.jpg -r %s -vcodec libx264 -crf
20 -g 15 -vf crop=2592:1458,scale=1280:720
timelapse.mp4"%(FPS_IN,'%5d',FPS_OUT))
```

It will take time varying from a few minutes to a few hours depending on the number of frames captured and the quality of the video, so be patient while working on this project.

To make it more understandable, here is the line-by-line explanation of the preceding script:

```
import os
import time
```

This will import two libraries: os and time. os will allow you to interact with the command line and time will enable you to set the time interval between frames:

```
FRAMES = 200
FPS_IN = 10
FPS_OUT = 25
WAITTIME = 10
FILMLENGTH = float(FRAMES / FPS_IN)
```

This will create five global variables. You already know what a global variable is and why it is used; however, just to reiterate, global variables can make your code more readable. By changing the value at one location, it will appear all through your program.

- **FRAMES**: This sets the number of images you will capture and add to your video.

- **FPS_IN**: This sets the number of the **frames per second** (**FPS**) that go into the video.

- **FPS_OUT**: This sets the FPS of the video created, that is, it creates a video running at 25 FPS. If FPS_IN is less that FPS_OUT, some FPS_IN frames will be used several times to bring the number up to FPS_OUT. 25 is a good value for a digital video.

- **WAITTIME**: This states the time (in seconds) between the frames that you are shooting with your camera. The Raspberry Pi camera takes roughly 6-8 seconds to take an image, so 8 seconds is the shortest time between shots.

- **FILMLENGTH**: This works out how long your film will be in seconds.

Let's take a look at the following code:

```
frameCount = 0
while frameCount< FRAMES:
   imageNumber = str(frameCount).zfill(5)
```

Once you have set the global variables, you want to capture and save images as per the value of global variable FRAMES. For this, a `while` loop is required, which will run until the required FRAMES are not captured and saved. imageNumber stores the string of the value in frameCount. Then, using the `.zfill(5)` method, you will get a string with 5 digits by filling all the preceding digits with a zero if there are not enough numbers. For example 1 becomes 00001 and 12 becomes 00012. Let's take a look at the following code:

```
os.system("raspistill -o image%s.jpg"%(imageNumber))
```

This will take the image using the `raspistill` tool and save it in the current folder. As you know `raspistill` is a command-line tool, you need some method in your Python code to access the command line. `os.system` will do the job for you. You will notice there is a `%s` with `%(imageNumber)` after the text. This says take whatever value is there in imageNumber and put it in place of `%s` while executing. So, images will get saved as `image00001.jpg`. You don't want to run the `while` loop infinitely, so increment frameCount once the picture is taken:

```
frameCount += 1
```

As I mentioned earlier, the Raspberry Pi camera takes 6-7 seconds to take an image, so if you want your camera to wait for 10 seconds, you need to put sleep time as (TIMEBETWEEN -6):

```
time.sleep(TIMEBETWEEN - 6) #Takes roughly 6 seconds to take a
picture
```

Like `raspistill`, avconv requires to be run on the command line and `os.system` will do the work for you. Most of the things you already know from the previous section.

```
os.system("avconv -r %s -i image%s.jpg -r %s -vcodec libx264 -crf
20 -g 15 -vf crop=2592:1458,scale=1280:720
timelapse.mp4"%(FPS_IN,'%5d',FPS_OUT))
```

However, here are some of the things that you should know.

First, `-r %'`; this will take the `FPS_IN` global variable value in place of `%s`.

`-I image%s.jpg`: These are input images that need to be used to create videos. Here, `%s` will take the value from `%5d`, which iterates through a five-digit number.

Second, `-r %s`; this will take the `FPS_OUT` global variable value in place of `%s`.

`-vf`: This is something that you haven't used before. vf stands for video filters. The Raspberry Pi camera provides images in the default size 2592*1944, and you might want to crop images and make the standard 1280*720 resolution video. In this case, there are two filters used. First, one will crop the incoming image to 2592*1458, and then filter scale them to 1280*720.

Developing a Twitter-controlled Raspberry Pi camera

In today's connected world, you want to access all of your things from everywhere. In *Chapter 4*, *Getting into Robotics*, you developed one such project where you can access and control your robot from anywhere using any devices. In this section, you will develop a Twitter-enabled Raspberry Pi camera, which will take a picture whenever you want to just by tweeting it.

Setting up

Before you start developing a Twitter-enabled Raspberry Pi camera, you need to have a Python library for accessing Twitter API on your Raspberry Pi, and of course, a few developer keys. The user has to send a direct message to the application developer, and then, it will analyze the direct message. If the direct message is from a valid user and in a valid format, it will take a picture from the camera. Once the picture has been taken, it will send the direct message to the user with the message, **I have taken the photo**. So, here are the two most important things in the setup process:

- Setting up Raspberry Pi
- Getting Twitter Access keys

Setting up Raspberry Pi

You need to install the Python library to access Twitter API on Raspberry Pi. Tweepy is an easy-to-use Python library to access the Twitter API. The easiest way to install the latest version is by using `pip/easy_install` to pull it from PyPI.Use the following command to install tweepy:

```
Sudo pip install tweepy
```

That's it! You have already used the Raspberry Pi camera before, so no other setup is required.

Getting Twitter Access keys

In this section, you will learn how to set up a Twitter developer account/application and get all access keys for reading/writing direct messages. Follow these steps to get all Twitter access keys that are required for this project:

NOTE: You don't necessarily have to do this on Raspberry Pi. You can use any computer with an Internet connection for getting the required licenses.

1. Go to `https://www.twitter.com` and log in using your credentials.

 Whoever logs in at `https://www.twitter.com` in step 1 will be a developer for the account and he will not be able to access the Raspberry Pi camera using tweets.

2. Go to `https://apps.twitter.com`, you will get a similar screen on your window. Click on the **Create New App** button provided on the top-right corner:

3. You will be redirected to another form where you can fill in your app details:

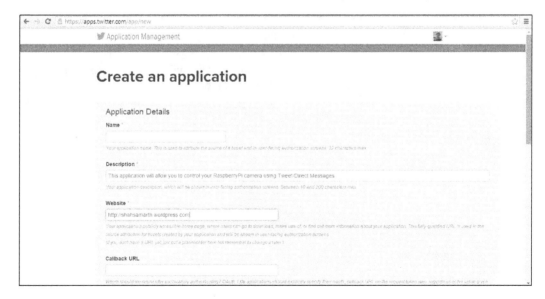

- ○ **Name**: This is your unique application name. You can give any name of your choice

- ○ **Description**: Here, you can write about your application. For example,
  ```
  This application will allow you to control your
  Raspberry Pi camera using Tweet/Direct Messages
  ```

- ○ **Website**: For now, you can put any placeholder. I have used my blog address.

4. Once you fill in all the details, scroll down and accept the developer agreement by checking the **Yes, I agree** checkbox. Then, click on **Create your Twitter application**:

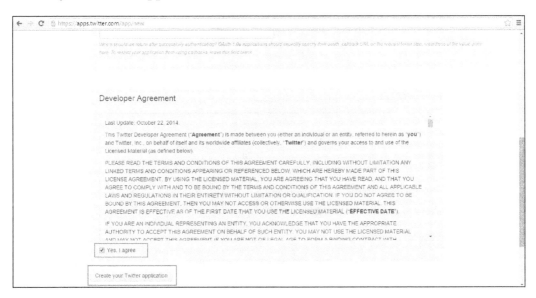

5. Now, your application is created. However, you will require a few more details such as reading/writing/access direct message permission as you need to access direct messages, and once you have captured the image, you need to send the direct message to the owner. Click on **Read only (modify app permissions)** under **Application Settings | Access level**:

6. Select the **Read, Write and Access direct messages** radio button, and then click on the **Update Settings** button:

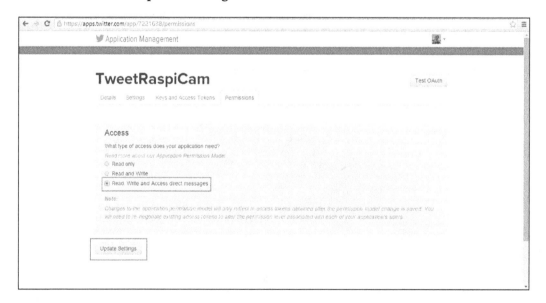

7. You will get a success message saying **The permission settings have been successfully updated. It may take a moment for the changes to reflect**. Click on the **Key and Access Tokens** tab.

8. You have to regenerate the application consumer key and keep it secret because the application permission has been modified. Click on the **Regenerate Consumer Key and Secret** button under **Application Actions**:

9. Now you will be asked for a confirmation whether you want to regenerate the keys. Click on the **Regenerate Consumer Key and Secret** button. Once the new key has been generated, you will be redirected to the success page:

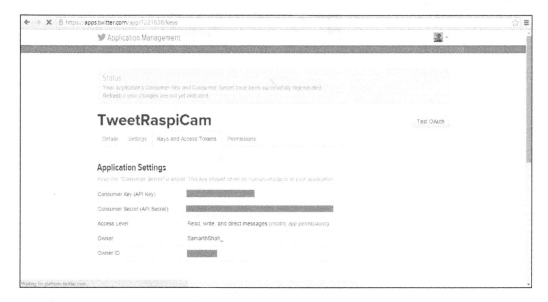

10. Scroll down this page, go to the **Your Access Token** section, and click on **Create my access token** under **Token Actions**:

11. Once the access token is generated, you will be redirected to the success page. Note down **Consumer Key(API Key)**, **Consumer Secret (API Secret)** under **Application Settings**, and **Access token**, **Access token secret** under **You access token**:

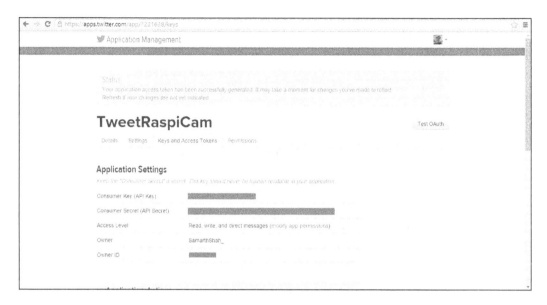

That's it.

Scripting

Following are the required steps to script a Twitter-controlled Raspberry Pi camera:

Go to the chapter5 folder on your Raspberry Pi by executing the following command in your terminal:

cd chapter5

Create a new Python file, tweetCam.py, inside that folder by executing the following command:

nano tweetCam.py

Copy the following code to your Python file:

```
import os
import time
import tweepy
```

```
USER="UserID"
LAST_MESSAGE_ID=0
MESSAGE_NUMBER='2'
DM_MESSAGE1="#TweetCam"
DM_MESSAGE2="Take Picture"
SLEEP_TIME=60

auth = tweepy.OAuthHandler(consumer_key,consumer_secret)
auth.set_access_token(access_token, access_token_secret)

api = tweepy.API(auth)
imageNumber=0
while(True):
  test=api.direct_messages(count=MESSAGE_NUMBER)
  for count in range(0,len(test)):
    if(LAST_MESSAGE_ID<test[count].id and
    test[count].sender_screen_name==USER and
    (test[count].text==DM_MESSAGE1 or
    test[count].text==DM_MESSAGE2)):
      os.system("raspistill -o image%d.jpg"%(imageNumber))
      api.send_direct_message(user=USER,text='I have taken the
      photo')
      LAST_MESSAGE_ID=test[count].id
      imageNumber+=1
  print("waittime")
  time.sleep(60)
```

You must be wondering how only few lines of code can do the magic. In this case, Tweepy is doing the magic by providing an easy-to-use Twitter API. Before you start executing your script, make sure you have understood the preceding code. Here is the line-by-line explanation of the preceding script:

```
import os
import time
import tweepy
```

This line will import the required Python library. Like the previous project, in this project, you will need to execute some code in the command line, and for this, the os module is imported in the first line. For setting the time difference between two Twitter API calls time module is imported. Finally, most importantly, tweepy module is imported for accessing the Twitter API. In this section, all the required Global variables are set:

```
USER="USERID"
LAST_MESSAGE_ID=0
MESSAGE_NUMBER='2'
```

```
DM_MESSAGE1="#TweetCam"
DM_MESSAGE2="Take Picture"
SLEEP_TIME=60
```

USER has the value of USERID who can access the Raspberry Pi camera using Tweets/direct messages.

LAST_MESSAGE_ID stores the ID of the last message read so that the script will not read the same message again.

MESSAGE_NUMBER sets the number of direct messages that you want to retrieve. You can set it to 1 to get the last direct message received.

DM_MESSAGE1 sets the direct message format using which the user has to sent the direct message.

DM_MESSAGE2 sets the direct message format using which the user has to send the direct message. This is the same as DM_MESSAGE1. Later in the code, you will come to know that the user can send a direct message in any of the two preceding formats.

SLEEP_TIME sets the interval after which it should again look for new direct messages.

Let's take a look at the next set of code:

```
auth = tweepy.OAuthHandler(consumer_key,consumer_secret)
auth.set_access_token(access_token, access_token_secret)

api = tweepy.API(auth)
```

The first two lines are the Twitter authentication lines that are required to prevent an unauthenticated user from getting access to user Twitter data. You have to put your consumer_key, consumer_secret, access_token, and access_token_secret at the respective fields mentioned in the preceding code in a single quote. The forth line creates an tweepy object by using the authentication data provided in the first two lines. Now, this object can be used for further processing:

```
imageNumber=0
```

Initially, imageNumber is set to 0. You don't want to overwrite the same image with new data when a new direct message is received. Later in the code, when one image is saved, the imageNumber value will get incremented by 1 so that new images are saved with a different name. Let's take a look at the next set of code:

```
while(True):
  test=api.direct_messages(count=MESSAGE_NUMBER)
  for count in range(0,len(test)):
```

```
        if(LAST_MESSAGE_ID<test[count].id and
        test[count].sender_screen_name==USER and
        (test[count].text==DM_MESSAGE1 or
        test[count].text==DM_MESSAGE2)):
            os.system("raspistill -o image%d.jpg"%(imageNumber))
            api.send_direct_message(user=USER,text='I have taken the
            photo')
            LAST_MESSAGE_ID=test[count].id
            imageNumber+=1
    print("waittime")
    time.sleep(60)
```

Now, you would want to run an infinite loop so that it keeps on checking when a new direct message from the user is available. `api.direct_message` is the tweepy method that will get the user messages received by the authenticated users. This method takes several parameters; however, in the preceding code only one parameter count is used to get the specific number (MESSAGE_NUMBER) of direct messages. Once you receive this, you run a `for` loop over the number of messages received. Before you call the Raspberry Pi method to take the picture, you need to verify the following:

- That this is the new message and not something for which you have already taken the picture

- This was send by an authenticated USER

- A direct message is in the correct format

Once all the verification has been done, you can take a picture using a Raspberry Pi camera. Similar to the previous project, `os.command` is used to execute the `raspistill` command. This will save an image by appending `imageNumber` at the end of the image name. Once the picture has been taken, it will send the direct message to the USER that **I have taken that Photo**. It was done using the `api.send_direct_message` method. Once the picture has been taken for a particular message, you need to save its ID to LAST_MESSAGE_ID so that you don't take the picture for the same direct message again. To give a different name for a different image, you need to increment `imageNumber`. Finally, once all the processes has been done, you will have to wait for SLEEP_TIME. For the preceding script, it is 60 seconds. After 60 seconds, it will fetch MESSAGE_NUMBER messages and start analyzing those messages.

Summary

In this chapter, image processing concepts were introduced, which were used in the later part of the chapter while working with image processing library OpenCV. In the later part of this chapter, the time-lapse video camera and the Twitter-controlled camera were developed.

In the next chapter, an advanced image processing algorithm will be introduced. Some of the well-known image processing problems such as face detection and background subtraction based projects will get developed.

6
Image Processing Algorithms

As mentioned in the previous chapter, image processing has become an integral part of our society, and whether you notice or not, it is being used everywhere. In the previous chapter, you learned about the basics of image processing and developed a couple of interesting projects using Raspberry Pi. One of the important guiding principles for image processing is: *If the eye can do it, so can the machines*. Thus, if an object is fairly well hidden in an image, yet the eye can see it and track it, then it should be possible to devise a vision algorithm that can do the same. In this chapter, you will develop an algorithm for the things that can be easily done by human eye. In addition to this, you will learn algorithms for certain tasks that are difficult to do with human eye. In the later part of this chapter, you will develop an interesting surveillance project from what you have learned so far. Here are the key topics that you will learn in this chapter:

- Important image processing operations
- Core algorithms
- Machine learning
- Projects

Important image processing operations

In the previous chapter, you learned about the basic image processing operations. This section will cover an important image processing operation, which is widely used in complex image processing algorithms:

- The image smoothing filter
- Morphological operations

The image smoothing filter

Image smoothing is used to remove the noise. Basically, it removes high frequency contents from the image. Noise and sharp edges are typically high frequency contents. As it removes edges along with the noise from an image, it will blur the image. OpenCV has mainly four types of smoothing filters:

- Averaging filter
- Gaussian filtering
- Median filtering
- Bilateral filtering

Averaging

The averaging technique takes the average of all the pixels under the kernel area and replaces the central element with this average. This can be achieved using `cv2.blur()` or `cv2.boxFilter()` functions. The following are the steps to achieve averaging:

1. Create a new folder named `chapter6` under your `home` folder.

2. Open the terminal window:

   ```
   cd ~
   mkdir chapter6
   ```

3. Create a new file named `averaging.py` in this folder:

   ```
   nano averaging.py
   ```

4. Write the following code to the `averaging.py` file:

   ```python
   import cv2
   import numpy as np
   img = cv2.imread('fly.jpg') # Read the original image
   blur = cv2.blur(img,(5,5)) #Blurred image ( Averaged Image) with
   kernel of 5*5
   cv2.imshow("Original" , img ) # Show original image
   cv2.imshow("Averaging" , blur ) # Show averaged image
   cv2.waitKey(0)
   cv2.destroyAllWindows()
   ```

The following image shows the original and averaged image side by side:

Gaussian filtering

In averaging filtering, all the coefficients of the kernel are equal, but in the case of Gaussian filtering, you can specify the standard deviation in X and Y directions. For example, the preceding code from the *Averaging* section can be updated for Gaussian filtering as follows:

```
import cv2
import numpy as np
img = cv2.imread('fly.jpg') # Read the original image
blur = cv2.GaussianBlur(img,(5,5),0) #Gaussian Blurred image with
5*5 kernal
cv2.imshow("Original" , img ) # Show original image
cv2.imshow("Gaussian Filter" , blur ) # Show Gaussian Filtered
image
cv2.waitKey(0)
cv2.destroyAllWindows()
```

In the previous example, only a standard deviation in the X direction is mentioned. In this case, the standard deviation in the Y direction is taken as the same as of the standard deviation in the X direction. Gaussian filtering is highly effective in removing Gaussian noise from the image. The following image shows the original and Gaussian filtered images side by side:

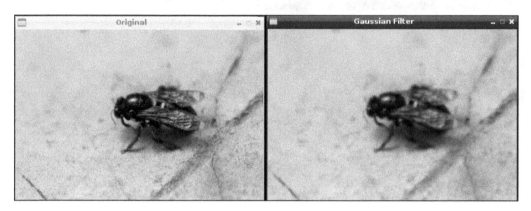

Median filtering

As the name suggests, it takes the median of all the pixels under the kernel window and the central pixel is replaced with this median value. This is highly effective in removing salt-and-pepper noise.

 In salt-and-pepper noise, a certain amount of the pixels in the image are either black or white (hence, the name of the noise).

In the previous two filters (Averaging and Gaussian), the filtered value for the central element can be a value that may not exist in the original image. However, this is not the case in median filtering, since the central element is always replaced by some pixel value in the image. This reduces the noise effectively. For example, the previous code from the *Gaussian filtering* section can be updated for median filtering as follows:

```
import cv2
import numpy as np
img = cv2.imread('fly.jpg') # Read the original image
median = cv2.medianBlur(img,5) #Median Blur with 5*5 kernel
cv2.imshow("Original" , img ) # Show original image
cv2.imshow("Median Filter" , median) # Show Median Filtered image
cv2.waitKey(0)
cv2.destroyAllWindows()
```

The following image shows the original and median filtered images side by side:

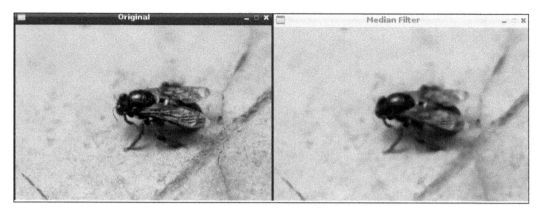

Bilateral filtering

As you can see from the previous results for all the three filters, it tends to remove the edges along with the noise. Bilateral filtering is highly effective at noise removal while preserving the edges of the image. This is similar to the Gaussian filter, but in a Gaussian filter, the weighted average is considered for all the points and it does not consider whether pixels lie on edges or not, while in bilateral filtering, apart from Gaussian filtering, one more filtering component is used, which is a function of pixel intensity differences. It will not include the pixels at the edges for the blurring. For example, the previous code from the *Median filtering* section can be updated for Bilateral filtering as follows:

```
import cv2
import numpy as np
img = cv2.imread('fly.jpg') # Read the original image
blur = cv2.bilateralFilter(img,9,75,75)
cv2.imshow("Original" , img ) # Show original image
cv2.imshow("Bilateral Filter" , blue) # Show Bilateral Filtered image
cv2.waitKey(0)
cv2.destroyAllWindows()
```

Here is the function that was used for bilateral filtering:

```
cv2.bilateralFilter(src,d,sigmaColor,sigmaSpace)
src - source image
d - Diameter of each pixel neighborhood that is used during
filtering
sigmaColor - Standard deviation in the color space.
sigmaSpace - Standard deviation in the coordinate space (in pixel
terms) ( Don't worry if you don't understand this )
```

The following image shows the original and bilateral filtered images side by side:

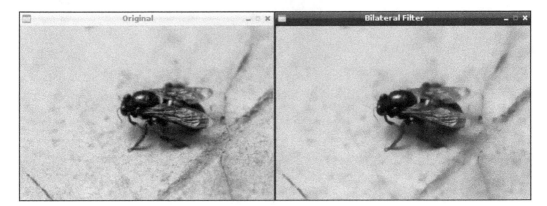

Morphological operations

The mathematical morphology is a theory and technique for the analysis and processing of geometrical structures. Morphological transformations are normally performed on binary images. It needs two inputs, one is an original image and the second one is called the structuring element or kernel, which decides the nature of operation. The basic morphological operators are erosion, dilation, opening, and closing.

Erosion

Erosion is similar to soil erosion. It erodes the boundaries of the foreground object. By now, you must be comfortable with kernels. In erosion, a pixel in the original image (either 1 or 0) will be considered 1, only if all the pixels under the kernel is 1; otherwise, it is eroded (made to zero). So, depending on the size of the kernel, all the points near the boundaries will get discarded. In other terms, the thickness of a foreground object decreases. To remove the small white noise and detaching two objects, erosion is used. Create a file named erosion.py under the chapter6 folder:

Write the following code to erosion.py:

```
import cv2
import numpy as np
img = cv2.imread("fly.jpg",0)
kernel = np.ones((5,5),np.uint8)
erosion = cv2.erode(img,kernel,iterations = 1)
cv2.imshow("Original" , img ) # Show original image
cv2.imshow("Erosion",erosion)
cv2.waitKey(0)
cv2.destroyAllWindows()
```

The following image shows the original and eroded images side by side:

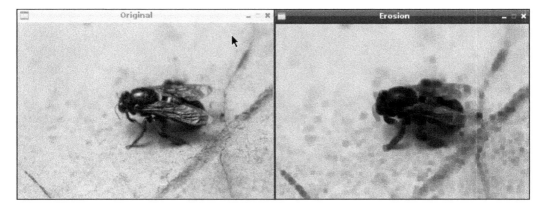

Dilation

Dilation is opposite of erosion. A pixel in the original image (either 1 or 0) will be considered 1 if any one pixel under the kernel is 1, so it increases the thickness of the foreground object. Mostly, in a noise removal scenario, erosion is followed by dilation because erosion removes the noise but at the same time shrinks the object. After the erosion, dilation will increase the thickness of the object, and as noise is gone, it won't come back. This is useful in joining broken part of the objects. For example, the previous code from *Erosion* can be updated for dilation as follows:

```
import cv2
import numpy as np
img = cv2.imread('fly.jpg,0)
kernel = np.ones((5,5),np.uint8)
dilation = cv2.dilate(img,kernel,iterations = 1)
cv2.imshow("Original" , img ) # Show original image
cv2.imshow("Dilation",dilation)
cv2.waitKey(0)
cv2.destroyAllWindows()
```

The following image shows the original and dilation image side by side:

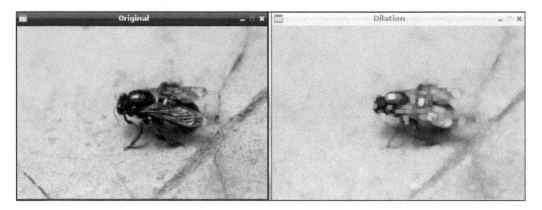

Opening

Opening is nothing but erosion followed by dilation. This is useful in removing noise. For example, the previous code from *Dilation* can be updated for opening as follows:

```
import cv2
import numpy as np
img = cv2.imread('opencv_logo.png',0)
kernel = np.ones((5,5),np.uint8)
opening = cv2.morphologyEx(img, cv2.MORPH_OPEN, kernel)
cv2.imshow("Original" , img ) # Show original image
cv2.imshow("Opening",opening)
cv2.waitKey(0)
cv2.destroyAllWindows()
```

The following image shows the original and opening images side by side:

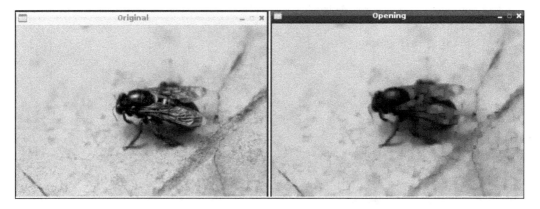

Closing

Closing is reverse of opening; dilation followed by erosion. This is useful in closing small holes inside a foreground object. For example, the preceding code can be updated for closing as shown here:

```
import cv2
import numpy as np
img = cv2.imread('fly.jpg',0)
kernel = np.ones((5,5),np.uint8)
closing = cv2.morphologyEx(img, cv2.MORPH_CLOSE, kernel)
cv2.imshow("Original" , img ) # Show original image
cv2.imshow("Closing",closing)
cv2.waitKey(0)
cv2.destroyAllWindows()
```

The following image shows the original and **Closing** images side by side:

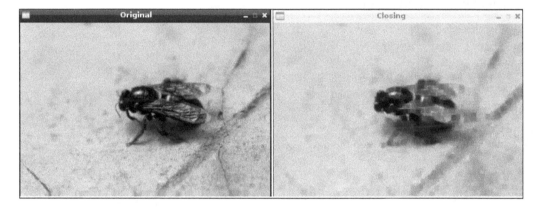

Core algorithms

In this section, you will learn about core image processing algorithms such as edge detection and background subtraction.

Edge detection

An edge may be defined as a set of connected pixels that forms a boundary between two disjoints regions. Edge detection is basically a method of segmenting an image into regions of discontinuity. Like many other core algorithms, there are many edge detection algorithms. In this section, you will get introduced to canny edge detection. This was developed by John F. Canny in 1986. This is a multistage algorithm.

All the stages of canny edge detection algorithm are explained in brief here: "Edge detection is susceptible to the noise in the image; the first step is to remove the noise in the image with a Gaussian filter, which was already described in the previous section. The second step is to find the intensity gradient of the image. After getting a gradient magnitude and direction, a full scan of the image is done to remove any unwanted pixels, which may not constitute the edge. As a result of this, you will get a binary image with thin edges. This step is called non-maximum suppression. The final stage hysteresis thresholding decides which all are really edges and which are not. For this, two threshold values, minVal and maxVal, are required. Any edges with a intensity gradient more than maxVal are sure to be edges and those below minVal are sure to be non-edges. Those who lie between these two thresholds are classified edges or non-edges based on their connectivity. If they are connected to "sure-edge" pixels, they are considered to be part of edges. Otherwise, they are also discarded."

OpenCV puts all the preceding lines in a single function, cv2.Canny(), so you don't have to worry about all other processing. Create a file named cannyEdgeDetection. py under the chapter6 folder:

```
import cv2
import numpy as np
img = cv2.imread('fly.jpg',0)
edges = cv2.Canny(img,100,200)
cv2.imshow("Original",img)
cv2.imshow("Edge Image",edges)
cv2.waitKey(0)
cv2.destrolAllWindows()


cv2.Canny(img,100,200)
First Argument - input image (img)
Second Argument - Minimum Threshold value (minValue)
Third Argument - Maximum Threshold value(maxValue)
```

There are two more parameters, but the preceding details will work in the context of this book.

The following image shows the original and canny edge image side by side:

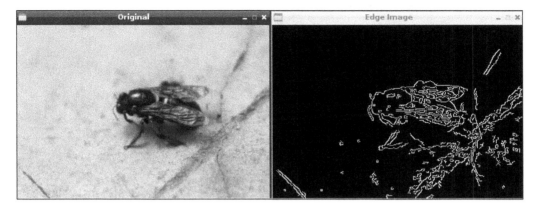

Background subtraction

Consider scenarios such as a visitor counter where a static camera takes the number of visitors entering or leaving the room, or a traffic camera extracting information about the vehicles. In all the cases, first you need to extract the visitor or vehicle alone. In technical terms, you need to extract the moving foreground from the background. That's where the background subtraction algorithm comes into play.

If you have an image of the background alone, then it will be easy to get the moving foreground object. For example, if you have an image of the room without visitors and an image of the roads without vehicles, you can just subtract the new image from the background and you will get the foreground object. However, in most of the scenarios, you don't have the background image, so it becomes challenging. It becomes more challenging when there is a shadow of the moving object in the image.

OpenCV has three algorithms for this purpose. In this chapter, you will implement two of those algorithms.

BackgroundSubtractorMOG

BackgroundSubtractorMOG is a Gaussian mixture-based background/foreground segmentation algorithm. In your code, you need to create a background object using the `cv2.BackgroundSubtractorMOG()` function. There are some optional parameters to this function:

Create a filename called `backgroundSubtractorMOG.py` inside the `chapter6` folder. Here is the code that you need to write to the file:

```python
import numpy as np
import cv2
cap = cv2.VideoCapture('unimore.avi') #Make sure you have video in
your current folder
backgroundObject = cv2.BackgroundSubtractorMOG()
while(1):
  ret, frame = cap.read()
  bg = backgroundObject.apply(frame)
  cv2.imshow('frame',bg)
  k = cv2.waitKey(30) & 0xff
  if k == 27:
    break
cap.release()
cv2.destroyAllWindows()
```

The following image shows the background subtracted image side by side with the original image:

The preceding code is explained in detail here:

```python
import numpy as np
import cv2
```

The preceding lines will import the required Python module. The following line of code will create a `VideoCapture` object with the given filename as a reference to the video:

```python
cap = cv2.VideoCapture('unimore.avi') #Make sure you have video in
your current folder
```

The following line of code will create an object of BackgroundSubstractorMOG:

```
backgroundObject = cv2.BackgroundSubtractorMOG()
```

Let's take a look at the following code:

```
while(1):
    ret, frame = cap.read()
    bg = backgroundObject.apply(frame)
    cv2.imshow('frame',bg)
    k = cv2.waitKey(30) & 0xff
    if k == 27:
        break
```

while(1) will create an infinite loop. cap.read() returns a Boolean value (true/false). If the frame is read correctly, it will be True. The bg = backgroundObject.apply(frame) statement will apply the BackgroundSubtractorMOG function to the frame that was read recently and store it in a variable called bg. The cv2.imshow('frame',bg) statement will show the background subtracted image. cv2.waitKey(30) will wait for 30 milliseconds for the user's input. & 0xff will help store only least 8 significant bit to the variable k. If the user entered key is ESC (27 ASCII value), then stop the execution. Let's take a look at the remaining part of the code:

```
cap.release()
cv2.destroyAllWindows()
```

cap.release() will release the object and cv2.destroyAllWindows() will close all the window that was created by this application.

BackgroundSubtractorMOG2

BackgroundSubtractorMOG2 is also a Gaussian mixture-based background/ foreground segmentation algorithm. In this algorithm, you have an option of selecting whether the shadow should be detected or not. If detectShadows = True, it detects and marks shadows, but decreases the speed. The shadows will be marked in gray color.

This example works only with OpenCV 2.4.9 and higher. If you have used Approach 1 for installing OpenCV on Raspberry Pi, check your OpenCV version. If it is below 2.4.9, you may skip this example.

You can use the same code that you have written in the previous algorithm. This is just that you have to create the backgroundSubtractor object using cv2.BackgroundSubtractorMOG2() instead of cv2.cBackgroundSubtractorMOG():

```python
import numpy as np
import cv2
cap = cv2.VideoCapture('unimore.avi')
backgroundObject = cv2.BackgroundSubtractorMOG2()
while(1):
    ret, frame = cap.read()
    mask = backgroundObject.apply(frame)
    cv2.imshow('frame',mask)
    k = cv2.waitKey(30) & 0xff
    if k == 27:
        break
cap.release()
cv2.destroyAllWindows()
```

The following image shows the result of the preceding code:

Machine learning

Like humans learn from their day-to-day activities, a machine or computer can also learn from the data that they are getting. The scientific area that explores the construction and exploration of such algorithms is called machine learning. In this section, you will learn about machine learning-based object detection algorithms, or more specifically, face detection and eye detection algorithms.

Object detection algorithm

In 2001, Viola and Jones proposed an effective object detection method for using Haar feature-based cascade classifiers. As mentioned earlier, it is a machine learning-based object detection method. You will require lots of positive images (images with an object to detect) and negative images (images without the object to detect) to train the classifier. Once you have many positive and negative images, you need to extract the features from it, but extracting all the features from the image and selecting the best features from the image would require extensive computation. This problem can be solved using AdaBoost in which after applying a feature on all the training images, based on some threshold value, images get classified into "With Object" and "Without Object". Of course, there will be some misclassification in this. There is some gain in terms of computation requirement with this setup, but again checking all the image window with all (reduced) features is a bit time consuming. In an image, most of the image region is a "Non-Object" region. So, it is a better idea to have a simple method to check whether a window is not a "Object" region. If it is not, discard it in a single shot. Don't process it again. Instead focus on a region where there can be a "Object". For this, they introduced the concept of cascade of classifiers. Instead of applying all the features on a window, group the features into different stages of classifiers and apply one by one. Normally, the first few stages will contain very less number of features. If a window fails the first stage, discard it. If it passes, apply the second stage of features and continue the process. The window that will pass all the classifiers contains the "object". This is the simple explanation of Viola-Jones algorithm from `http://opencv-python-tutroals.readthedocs.org/en/latest/py_tutorials/py_objdetect/py_face_detection/py_face_detection.html`. Refer to their research paper for more detailed explanation.

Face detection

The Viola-Jones algorithm can be used for any object detection. In this section, you will use it to detect faces in the image. OpenCV comes with a detector as well as trainer. In this section, you will not train the Haar classifier to detect faces. Instead you will use the pre-trained classifier for face. This classifier (XML file) for face can be found in the `opencv/data/haarcascades/` directory.

> If you want to train your own classifier for detecting other objects such as car, planes, and ball, refer to `http://docs.opencv.org/doc/user_guide/ug_traincascade.html` for detailed explanation.

Create a file `faceDetection.py` inside the `chapter6` folder.

Here is the complete code:

```
import numpy as np
import cv2
face_cascade =
cv2.CascadeClassifier('haarcascade_frontalface_default.xml') #
You can get the xml file from book website under code bundles.
img = cv2.imread('samarth.jpg')
gray = cv2.cvtColor(img, cv2.COLOR_BGR2GRAY)
faces = face_cascade.detectMultiScale(gray, 1.3, 5)
for (x,y,w,h) in faces:
  cv2.rectangle(img,(x,y),(x+w,y+h),(255,0,0),2)
cv2.imshow('img',img)
cv2.waitKey(0)
cv2.destroyAllWindows()
```

The following image shows the result of the preceding code:

The preceding code is explained in detail as follows:

```
import numpy as np
import cv2
```

The preceding lines will import the required Python module. The following line of code will load the trained classifier of the frontal face from the haarcascade_frontalface_default.xml file. It will return a cascadeClassifier object to face_cascade variable:

```
face_cascade =
cv2.CascadeClassifier('haarcascade_frontalface_default.xml')
```

The following line of code will load an image on which this algorithm needs to be run:

```
img = cv2.imread('samarth.jpg')
```

The following line of code will convert the loaded image into a grayscale image:

```
gray = cv2.cvtColor(img, cv2.COLOR_BGR2GRAY)
```

The following line of code will detect objects of different sizes in the input image:

```
faces = face_cascade.detectMultiScale(gray, 1.3, 5)
```

The detected objects are returned as a list of rectangles. Here, the second and third parameters are scaleFactor and minNeighbours, respectively:

- scaleFactor: This is a parameter specifying how much the image size is reduced at each image scale
- minNeighbors: This is a parameter specifying how many neighbors each candidate rectangle should have to retain the current rectangle candidate

The following line of code will run for all the faces detected:

```
for (x,y,w,h) in faces:
    cv2.rectangle(img,(x,y),(x+w,y+h),(255,0,0),2)
```

The cv2.rectangle(img,(x,y),(x+w,y+h),(255,0,0),2) statement will draw a rectangle between (x,y) top left and (x+w,y+h) bottom right will red color (255,0,0) with thickness of 2 pixels. Let's take a look at the remaining lines of code:

```
cv2.imshow('img',img)
cv2.waitKey(0)
cv2.destroyAllWindows()
```

The preceding lines of code will display the result image and wait for user input infinitely. Once user inputs are received, it will close all the windows created by this application.

Eye detection

In the previous section, you developed a Python application that can detect the faces in the image. In this section, you will expand the same code and use it to detect eyes. Similar to the previous section, here also you will use a pretrained classifier for eyes. Here is the complete code for eye detection:

```
import numpy as np
import cv2
face_cascade = cv2.CascadeClassifier('haarcascade_frontalface_default.
xml')
eye_cascade = cv2.CascadeClassifier('haarcascade_eye.xml')
img = cv2.imread('samarth.jpg')
gray = cv2.cvtColor(img, cv2.COLOR_BGR2GRAY)
faces = face_cascade.detectMultiScale(gray, 1.3, 5)
for (x,y,w,h) in faces:
    cv2.rectangle(img,(x,y),(x+w,y+h),(255,0,0),2)
    roi_gray = gray[y:y+h, x:x+w]
    roi_color = img[y:y+h, x:x+w]
    eyes = eye_cascade.detectMultiScale(roi_gray)
    for (ex,ey,ew,eh) in eyes:
        cv2.rectangle(roi_color,(ex,ey),(ex+ew,ey+eh),(0,255,0),2)
cv2.imshow('img',img)
cv2.waitKey(0)
cv2.destroyAllWindows()
```

The following image shows the result of the following code:

Most of the code should be self-explanatory as it is derived from a face detection application. However, there are a couple of lines that were added, which are explained as follows:

```
eye_cascade = cv2.CascadeClassifier('haarcascade_eye.xml')
```

The preceding line of code will load the trained classifier of eye from the `haarcascade_eye.xml` file. It will return an `cascadeClassifier` object to the `eye_cascade` variable. Let's take a look at the following lines of code:

```
for (x,y,w,h) in faces:
    cv2.rectangle(img,(x,y),(x+w,y+h),(255,0,0),2)
    roi_gray = gray[y:y+h, x:x+w]
    roi_color = img[y:y+h, x:x+w]
    eyes = eye_cascade.detectMultiScale(roi_gray)
    for (ex,ey,ew,eh) in eyes:
        cv2.rectangle(roi_color,(ex,ey),(ex+ew,ey+eh),(0,255,0),2)
```

For detecting the eye, you don't have to run the classifier on a whole image instead you can run in on the detected face. `roi_gray` will store the gray region that you should use for the eye detection algorithm. Similarly, `roi_color` will have the color region that you should use for the eye detection algorithm. Similar to `face_cascade_detectMultiScale(gray)`, `eye_cascade.detectMultiScale(roi_gray)` returns all the detected eyes in the form of a rectangle. `cv2.rectangle(roi_color,(ex,ey),(ex+ew,ey+eh),(0,255,0),2)` draws a rectangle at `(ex,ey)` top left and `(ex+ew,ey+eh)` bottom right with green color `(0,255,0)` with a thickness of 2 pixels.

Projects

You must have noticed that throughout this book, in the initial section of the chapter, you learned something new and in the last section of the chapter will you solve few real-life problems by developing a prototype. Following this tradition, in this section, you will develop two prototypes. In this section, you will learn about the following topics:

- The track object position
- The case study of OpenRelief
- Twitter-enabled surveillance systems

The track object position

For an object, there are needs that you want to keep particular item at the same place where you have taken and in some cases you require precise information. In this section, you will develop an application that will find the position of a particular object (for example, a circular coin) and determine its offset in x, y and any rotation of the object. Consider a scenario where you want to keep two circular objects at a particular location.

As a starting point, here two circular objects are taken. Create a file named `objectPosition.py` inside the `chapter6` folder.

Here is the code that you need to write in `objectPosition.py` file:

```python
import os
import cv2
import math

##Resize with resize command
def resizeImage(img):
    dst = cv2.resize(img,None, fx=0.25, fy=0.25, interpolation =
    cv2.INTER_LINEAR)
    return dst

##Take image with Raspberry Pi camera
os.system("raspistill -o image.jpg")

##Load image
img = cv2.imread("/home/pi/Desktop/image.jpg")
gray = cv2.imread("/home/pi/Desktop/image.jpg",0) #0 for grayscale

##Run Threshold on image to make it black and white
ret, thresh = cv2.threshold(gray,50,255,cv2.THRESH_BINARY)

##Use houghcircles to determine centre of circle
circles = cv2.HoughCircles(thresh,cv2.cv.CV_HOUGH_GRADIENT,1,75,param1
=50,param2=13,minRadius=0,maxRadius=175)
for i in circles[0,:]:
    #draw the outer circle
    cv2.circle(img,(i[0],i[1]),i[2],(0,255,0),2)
    #draw the centre of the circle
    cv2.circle(img,(i[0],i[1]),2,(0,0,255),3)

##Determine co-ordinates for centre of circle
x1 = circles[0][0][0]
```

```
y1 = circles[0][0][1]
x2 = circles[0][1][0]
y2 = circles[0][1][1]

##Angle betwen two circles
theta = math.degrees(math.atan((y2-y1)/(x2-x1)))

##print information
print "x1 = ",x1
print "y1 = ",y1
print "x2 = ",x2
print "y2 = ",y2
print theta
print circles

##Resize image
img = resizeImage(img)
thresh = resizeImage(thresh)
##Show Images
cv2.imshow("thresh",thresh)
cv2.imshow("img",img)
cv2.waitKey(0)
```

Here is the result of the preceding code:

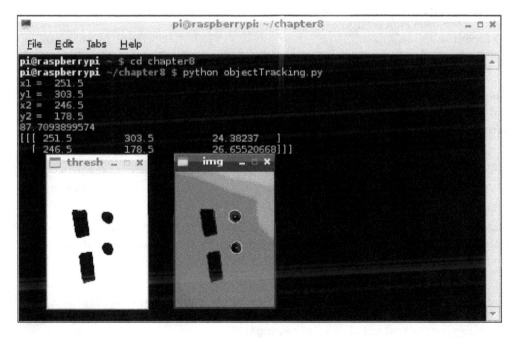

The following image shows the result of the previous algorithm running on the other image:

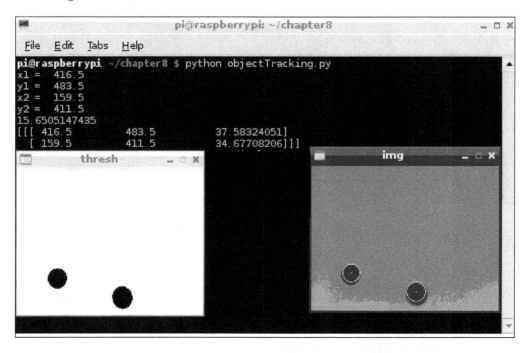

Here is a detailed explanation of the previous code:

```
import os
import cv2
import math
```

The preceding lines of code will import the three modules. Although you will do analysis on a full image, you need to make the images smaller for a proper display on the screen. The following lines will create a function named resizeImage():

```
def resizeImage(img):
    dst = cv2.resize(img,None, fx=0.25, fy=0.25, interpolation =
    cv2.INTER_LINEAR)
    return dst
```

Using os.system, you can input a command into the command line. raspistill -o image.jpg will take an image from the Raspberry Pi camera and store it as image. jpg in the current folder:

```
img - image that you want to resize
fx=0.25 and fy=0.25 are the factors that x and y are multiplied by.
0.25 makes the image 1/4 size.
os.system("raspistill -o image.jpg")
```

The following lines will load the image that was taken by the Raspberry Pi camera. `img` will have the color image and `gray` will have the grayscale image:

```
img = cv2.imread("/home/pi/Desktop/image.jpg")
gray = cv2.imread("/home/pi/Desktop/image.jpg",0)
ret, thresh = cv2.threshold(gray,50,255,cv2.THRESH_BINARY)
```

Using threshold function, you can convert your image into a binary image, as shown here:

```
Gray - the image that you want to convert
50 - It is a threshold value. It should be between 0 to 255 where
0 is white and 255 is black
255 - If a pixel is above threshold value , make it 255. Else it
is 0.
```

On the preceding binary image, you can run `HoughCircles` as follows:

```
circles =
cv2.HoughCircles(thresh,cv2.cv.CV_HOUGH_GRADIENT,1,75,param1=50,pa
ram2=13,minRadius=0,maxRadius=175)
```

`HoughCircle` returns *x* and *y* coordinates for each circle as well as the radius of the circle. These details are stored in circle variables, as shown here:

```
thresh - refers that you are running hough transform on the black
and white image.
75 - refers to the minimum distance allowed between circles.
Param1 = 50  This is one of the parameters which determines where
the circles are, you can play around with this figure if needs be.
Param2 = 13 If you are getting too many circles then increase this
number, and vice versa.The smaller it is, the more false circles
may be detected.
minRadius - the smallest radius allowed for a circle.
maxRadius - the largest radius allowed for a circle.
for i in circles[0,:]:
  #draw the outer circle
  cv2.circle(img,(i[0],i[1]),i[2],(0,255,0),2)
  #draw the centre of the circle
  cv2.circle(img,(i[0],i[1]),2,(0,0,255),3)
```

`cv2.circle(img,(i[0],i[1]),i[2],(0,255,0),2)` will draw the outer circle on the image img at `(i[0],i[1])` with the radius `i[2]` with green color `(0,255,0)` and thickness of 2 pixels. Similarly, `cv2.circle(img,(i[0],i[1]),2,(0,0,255),3)` will draw the center circle on the image img at `(i[0],i[1])` with the radius 2 with red color `(0,0,255)` and thickness of 3 pixels. Let's take a look at the following lines of code:

```
#Determine co-ordinates for center of circle
x1 = circles[0][0][0]
y1 = circles[0][0][1]
x2 = circles[0][1][0]
y2 = circles[0][1][1]
##Angle betwen two circles
theta = math.degrees(math.atan((y2-y1)/(x2-x1)))
```

The main application of this project is to find out the coordinate of the object (here, circle) and preceding lines of code to extract the coordinate of the two circles, and using simple trigonometry, the angle between two circles is calculated.

```
print "x1 = ",x1
print "y1 = ",y1
print "x2 = ",x2
print "y2 = ",y2
print theta
print circles
```

The preceding lines will print all the information that was calculated from the previous code. The following lines will make use of the `resizeImage` function that was created in the beginning of the program so that it will get displayed properly on the screen:

```
img = resizeImage(img)
thresh = resizeImage(thresh)
```

Now, let's look at the rest of the code:

```
cv2.imshow("thresh",thresh)
cv2.imshow("img",img)
cv2.waitKey(0)
```

There is no need of displaying the image as you have already printed all the information. However, for fault finding, it will be of good help.

OpenRelief

Planning disaster relief efforts is like trying to see through fog. OpenRelief is a project to develop better communications tools that will help clear this fog. This enables the right aid to get to the right places at the right time.

OpenRelief uses an open source approach that ensures everyone, anywhere, can access our technology. We are working to complement other projects around the world to support the emergence of open, humanitarian drone technology.

Capabilities

- Take off from footpaths
- Recognize roads, people, and smoke
- Photograph, film, and map the landscape
- Measure weather, radiation, and other conditions via modular sensors

Technical specifications

- Arduino Mega to fly the plane
- A super HAD CCD Fisheye camera to see
- Arduino-based sensors to gather information
- Raspberry Pi to process the data
- Raspian OS to analyze the results

 Building an OpenRelief kind of project is out of scope of this book. However, I have added some information as an inspiration of what can be done using Raspberry Pi in an image processing area.

For more details, refer to `http://www.openrelief.org/home/`.

Twitter-enabled surveillance systems

In this section, you will extend the work that you have done in the *Face detection* section. You will develop a Twitter-enabled surveillance system. The system will look for any intruder in your house and will send you a tweet with the current photograph when someone enters your house.

Create a filename `twitterSurveillance.py` in the folder named `chapter6` using this code:

```
import numpy as np
import cv2
import tweepy
import os
import time


# Consumer keys and access tokens, used for OAuth
consumer_key = 'copy your consumer key here'
consumer_secret = 'copy your consumer secret here'
access_token = 'copy your access token here'
access_token_secret = 'copy your access token secret here'

# OAuth process, using the keys and tokens
auth = tweepy.OAuthHandler(consumer_key, consumer_secret)
auth.set_access_token(access_token, access_token_secret)
api = tweepy.API(auth)
tweetUserID='USERID' #ENTER TWITTER HANDLE with @ here. For Example @
SamarthShah_
```

```
face_cascade = cv2.CascadeClassifier('haarcascade_frontalface_default.
xml') # You can get xml file from book website under code bundle
section
while True:
  os.system("raspistill -o image.jpg")
  cv2.waitKey(10)
  img = cv2.imread('/home/pi/chapter6/image.jpg')
  gray = cv2.imread('/home/pi/chapter6/image.jpg',0)
  faces = face_cascade.detectMultiScale(gray, 1.3, 5)
  for (x,y,w,h) in faces:
    cv2.rectangle(img,(x,y),(x+w,y+h),(255,0,0),2)
    # Send the tweet with photo
    photo_path = '/home/pi/chapter6/image.jpg'
    status = tweetUserID +'Photo tweet from Pi: ' +
    time.strftime('%Y/%m/%d %H:%M:%S')
    api.update_with_media(photo_path, status=status)
    time.sleep(60)
```

The following picture was taken by a Raspberry Pi camera:

I haven't installed the Raspberry Pi camera in my house. Instead ran the code in another environment and tested it.

Here is a detailed explanation of the previous code:

```
import numpy as np
import cv2
import tweepy
import os
import time
```

The preceding code will import the required Python modules. Let's take a look at the following code:

```
# Consumer keys and access tokens, used for OAuth
consumer_key = 'copy your consumer key here'
consumer_secret = 'copy your consumer secret here'
access_token = 'copy your access token here'
access_token_secret = 'copy your access token secret here'
```

These are the keys that are required for using the Twitter API. For getting these keys, please refer to *Getting Twitter Access keys* section in *Chapter 5, Introduction to Image Processing*. The following lines of code will create the tweepy object using the access key that was provided:

```
# OAuth process, using the keys and tokens
auth = tweepy.OAuthHandler(consumer_key, consumer_secret)
auth.set_access_token(access_token, access_token_secret)
api = tweepy.API(auth)
```

This `api` can be used to post the tweet to Twitter from Raspberry Pi. The following line of code will store the Twitter `UserID` of the user to whom the tweet should be sent when someone enters the house:

```
tweetUserID='USERID' #ENTER TWITTER HANDLE with @ here. For
Example @SamarthShah_
```

The following line of code will load the trained classifier for the face:

```
face_cascade =
cv2.CascadeClassifier('haarcascade_frontalface_default.xml')
```

The following line of code will take the picture from the Raspberry Pi camera:

```
os.system("raspistill -o /home/pi/chapter6/image.jpg")
cv2.waitKey(60)
```

As mentioned a couple of times in this book, `os.system` is used to execute the command in a command window. `raspistill` takes around 6 seconds to take the pictures, so `cv2.waitKey(60)` is used to stop the further execution of the program until the image has been saved. Let's take a look at the following lines of code:

```
img = cv2.imread('/home/pi/chapter6/image.jpg')
gray = cv2.imread('/home/pi/chapter6/image.jpg',0)
faces = face_cascade.detectMultiScale(gray, 1.3, 5)
```

This will read the image taken by the Raspberry Pi camera, and then using the `detectMultiScale` function of the `face_cascade` object, faces were detected and it gets stored in the `faces` variable. Let's take a look at the following lines of code:

```
for (x,y,w,h) in faces:
    cv2.rectangle(img,(x,y),(x+w,y+h),(255,0,0),2)
# Send the tweet with photo
    photo_path = '/home/pi/chapter6/image.jpg'
status = tweetUserID +' Photo tweet from Pi: ' +
time.strftime('%Y/%m/%d %H:%M:%S')
    api.update_with_media(photo_path, status=status)
    time.sleep(60)
```

Once the faces are detected for the detected face, a tweet will get sent to the user with `tweetUserID`. The `time.strftime('%Y/%m/%d %H:%M:%S')` statement will give the current time, which will also get sent to `tweetUserID`.

So, once you have started this program, if someone enters your home while you are out, the tweet will get sent to you with the image taken from the Raspberry Pi camera and the current time.

Summary

In this chapter, some image processing operations were explained in the first part of the chapter. Some of the widely used image processing algorithms were explained, and you understood how it can be used with Raspberry Pi. In the later part of the chapter, some of the interesting projects were developed using the algorithm explained earlier.

From a new learning perspective, this is the last chapter of the book. In the next chapter, common troubleshooting techniques will be mentioned.

7
Troubleshooting, Tips/Tricks, and Resources for Advanced Users

In this book, you were introduced to Raspberry Pi and its capability, you configured the LAMP server on Raspberry Pi, got introduced to electronics concepts, and finally, the basics of image processing and algorithm were developed and tested on Raspberry Pi. There might be instances when you wanted to know more about a certain topic or you were stuck in between. This chapter answers all those questions. In the first section, common troubleshooting techniques are mentioned. The second part of the chapter mentions some of the useful tips and tricks. Finally, the last part of this chapter has resources that will be useful if you want to go advanced with Raspberry Pi. We will cover the following topics in this chapter:

- Troubleshooting
- Tips and tricks
- Resources for advanced users

Troubleshooting

This section has answers to some of the common problems that you might face while working with Raspberry Pi.

Power/booting/installation

Raspberry Pi power supply is widely misunderstood. A lot of the problem is because of improper power supply. A power supply that can provide 5V and 1A is good enough. However, if you are planning to use a WiFi USB adapter other than what I had suggested, try using a 5V, 2A power supply, which can help Raspberry Pi run more stable.

> Raspberry Pi has no BIOS like your normal computer, so nothing will get displayed on screen unless Raspberry Pi successfully boots.

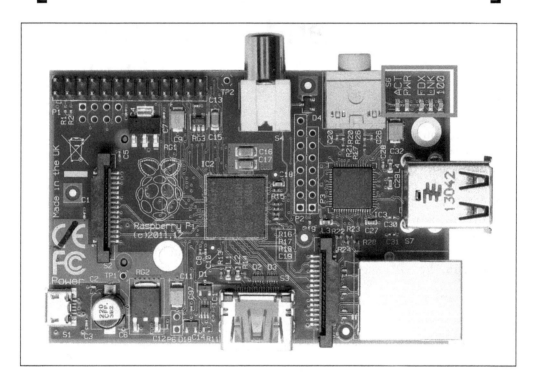

There are five LEDs near the USB connector. The status of these LEDs can help interpret the problem with a Raspberry Pi:

LED	Color	Function	Normal status
OK	Green	Card status	This will flash during an SD card activity
PWR	Red	Power	This will be steady ON when Raspberry Pi receives power

LED	Color	Function	Normal status
FDX	Orange	Full duplex	This will be ON when the Ethernet connection is fully duplex
LNK	Orange	Link	This will be ON when the Ethernet is connected
100	Orange	100 Mbps	This will be ON when connected to 100 Mbps

The LED status and their interpretation

The LED status and their interpretation is as follows:

The red Power LED does not turn ON, nothing gets displayed on screen

This means your power is not properly connected. Check the power supply connection and try again.

The red power LED is blinking

Raspberry Pi is getting power, but this is not sufficient. Use a different power supply.

The red power LED is ON, the green LED does not flash, and nothing gets displayed on screen

This means one of the following things:

- Raspberry Pi is getting a proper power supply, but the SD card is not inserted. Check the SD card status and try again.

- Raspberry Pi is getting a proper power supply, but the SD card is not connected properly. Check the SD card status and try again.

- Raspberry Pi is getting a proper power supply, the SD card is inserted properly, but there is no valid image on the SD card (make sure you have installed a valid OS on the SD card).

- Raspberry Pi is getting a proper power supply, the SD card is inserted properly, but it is corrupted. Use a different SD card, load the OS, and try again.

- Raspberry Pi is taking too much power because of the connected peripherals. Remove all the peripherals and try again.

- The power supply in itself is not able to provide 5V power supply. Use a different power supply and try again.

The green LED blinks in a specific pattern

- 3 flashes :start.elf not found
- 4 flashes :start.elf not launched
- 7 flashes :kernel.img not found

In all the preceding cases, you need to reload the OS to SD card and try again. This will solve the problem.

A colored splash screen stays forever

A colored splash screen is displayed after start.elf is launched. This should get replaced by the Linux kernel when kernel.img is loaded, but if the colored splash screen is staying forever, Raspberry Pi cannot find kernel.img. Try replacing the SD card, reload the OS again to the SD card, and check again.

Kernel panic on boot

If you receive kernel panic on boot, it might occur because of the USB devices (keyboard, mouse, or any other devices) connected. Try removing the connected USB devices.

Raspberry Pi shuts down after booting up

If your Raspberry Pi shuts down after booting up, this might be because the power supply is not able to provide enough power to the Raspberry Pi board. Try replacing the power supply.

Inputs

Raspberry Pi does not respond to keyboard/mouse.

As mentioned earlier, most of the problem with Raspberry Pi is because of the inadequate power supply. In this case too, try using a good power supply and good cable. Some cheap cables that work with a cell phone cannot fully power the Raspberry Pi. There are USB devices that require more power. Check the voltage and current rating of the devices before connecting it to the Raspberry Pi USB port. If it is more than 5V 100mA, it is better to use USB hub to power such devices.

> I am using the Nokia Lumia 520 USB cable to power up Raspberry Pi. It is working fine with this USB cable.

USB webcam

You can use the following command to test your webcam with Raspberry Pi and change configuration settings if required:

```
sudo apt-get install guvcview
```

Based on the camera, it might work with an internal USB port only, not with an external USB hub.

Networking

Ethernet connects at 10M instead of 100M.

In rev.1.0, the LED corner is mislabeled with 10M instead of 100M. When that LED is ON, Raspberry Pi is connected to 100 Mbps.

The Ethernet connection is lost when any USB device is plugged in

The Raspberry Pi USB ports are configured in such a way that it can provide 100mA current to both the USB port. However, if you try to connect the USB device, which requires more current (>100 mA), then connect it using a powered USB hub.

Sound

Sound does not work with the HDMI monitor. This is caused by some computer monitors that select the DVI mode even if an HDMI cable is connected. This is required even if the other HDMI devices work perfectly with the same monitor.

Add the following line to the configuration file, `/boot/config.txt`:

```
hdmi_drive=2
```

The preceding line of code will force it to select the HDMI mode.

Sound does not work in some applications.

The Raspberry Pi OS also comes with drivers installed by default. However, to install support for sound, enter the following command in your command line:

```
sudo apt-get update
sudo apt-get upgrade
sudo apt-get install alsa-utils
sudo modprobe snd_bcm2835
```

Try entering the following command to test whether sound is working or not:

```
aplay /usr/share/sounds/alsa/Front_Center.wav
```

The Raspberry Pi camera

The camera board requires 250mA to operate. Make sure your power supply can provide enough power for the camera module as well as Raspberry Pi, and any peripherals directly attached to Raspberry Pi.

RaspiStill does not work, no image is taken

The Raspberry Pi camera is very simple to use. First, make sure that you have connected the camera as per the instruction mentioned in *Chapter 4*, *Getting into Robotics*. When the camera module is in use, you will see the red LED blinking on the module.

Display

If you just get errors instead of a desktop, when typing startx, you may be out of storage space on the SD card. gparted can expand a partition, if the SD card is less then 2 GB. Expanding the partition will solve the problem.

Firmware updates

The kernel and firmware are installed as a Debian package. These packages are updated infrequently after extensive testing. You can use the following command to update the Raspberry Pi firmware:

```
sudo apt-get update && sudo apt-get install rpi-update
```

Manual disk resize

The Raspbian wheezy image (as downloaded) only uses the first 2 GB of space on the SD card. There are two options. You can use the **Raspi-config** GUI to resize the disk or you can do it programmatically. The **expand_rootfs** menu item reconfigures the operating system to use all of the space available on the SD card. A restart is required to make the reconfigure take effect, as shown in the following image:

```
Raspi-config
        info                 Information about this tool
        expand_rootfs        Expand root partition to fill SD card
        overscan             Change overscan
        configure_keyboard   Set keyboard layout
        change_pass          Change password for 'pi' user
        change_locale        Set locale
        change_timezone      Set timezone
        memory_split         Change memory split
        overclock            Configure overclocking
        ssh                  Enable or disable ssh server
        boot_behaviour       Start desktop on boot?
        update               Try to upgrade raspi-config


               <Select>                     <Finish>
```

These are the steps to manually resize the disk:

1. From the command line or a terminal window, enter the following:

    `sudo fdisk /dev/mmcblk0`

2. Type p to list the partition table.

3. You should see three partitions. If you look in the last column labeled **System**, you should have:

    `W95 FAT32`

    `Linux`

    `Linux Swap`

4. Make a note of the start number for partition **2**, you will need this later.

5. Next, type d to delete a partition.

6. You will then be prompted for the number of the partition you want to delete. In the preceding case, you would want to delete both the Linux and Linux swap partitions, so type 2.

7. Then, type d again and then type 3 to delete the swap partition.

8. Now, you can resize the main partition. Type n to create a new partition.

9. This new partition needs to be a primary partition, so type p.

10. Next, enter 2 when prompted for a partition number.

11. You will now be prompted for the first sector for the new partition. Enter the start number from the earlier step (the Linux partition) (In my case it was 122880 which I got from Step 4).

12. Next, you will be prompted for the last sector; you can just hit *Enter* to accept the default value as this value can vary depending upon the memory card size, which will utilize the remaining disk space.

13. Type w to save the changes you made.

14. Next, reboot the system with the following command:

```
sudo reboot
```

15. Once the system reboots and you are back at the command line, enter the following command:

```
sudo resize2fs /dev/mmcblk0p2
```

Note that this can take a long time (depending on the card size and speed); be patient and let it finish so that you do not mess up the filesystem and have to start from scratch.

16. Once it is done, reboot the system with the following command:

```
sudo reboot
```

17. You can now verify that the system is using the full capacity of the SD card by entering the following command:

```
df -h
```

Tips and tricks

The previous section has the solution to most of the challenges that you might face while using this book. You should not limit your Raspberry Pi learning to what has been covered in this book. This section covers some interesting tips and tricks that will be useful to you.

Play MP3 files

The Raspbian OS contains the standard distribution to play .wav files. However, if you want to play MP3 files, install the mpg321 library by executing the following command in the terminal:

```
sudo apt-get update
sudo apt-get upgrade
sudo apt-get install mpg321
```

You can play MP3 files with the following command:

```
mpg321 "my file.mp3"
```

Remove boot messages

Go to the Raspberry Pi terminal and enter the following command:

```
cd /boot/
```

```
sudo nano cmdline.txt
```

At the end of the file, add this:

```
    loglevel=0
```

The preceding line would suppress every log from the kernel. Reboot the Raspberry Pi, still you will see some messages. To remove these messages, use the following code:

```
cd /boot/
```

```
sudo nano cmdline.txt
```

Change console =tty1 to console =tty4.

This will suppress all the boot messages except Raspberry Pi logo. Restart your Raspberry Pi to check the boot screen only with Raspberry Pi logo.

Remove the Raspberry Pi logo from boot screen

Go to the Raspberry Pi terminal and enter the following command:

```
cd /boot/
```

```
sudo nano cmdline.txt
```

Add logo.nologo at the end of the file.

Restart Raspberry Pi. You will notice that Raspberry Pi logo is not displayed on boot screen this time.

Remove unnecessary files from Raspberry Pi

You have to remove the unnecessary files from Raspberry Pi; otherwise, the SD card will eventually become full and you can't access it. Use the following command to remove unnecessary files from Raspberry Pi:

```
rm -rf ~/.local/share/Trash/files/*
```

Show all/hidden folders/file

Go to Raspberry Pi terminal and enter the following command:

```
ls-a
```

This will show all/hidden files of the current directory you are in.

Show a list of Python modules installed on systems

Go to Raspberry Pi terminal and enter the following command:

```
help('modules')
```

Raspberry Pi board info / CPU info

Go to Raspberry Pi terminal and enter the following command:

```
cat /proc/cpuinfo
```

The following screenshot is the result of the preceding command:

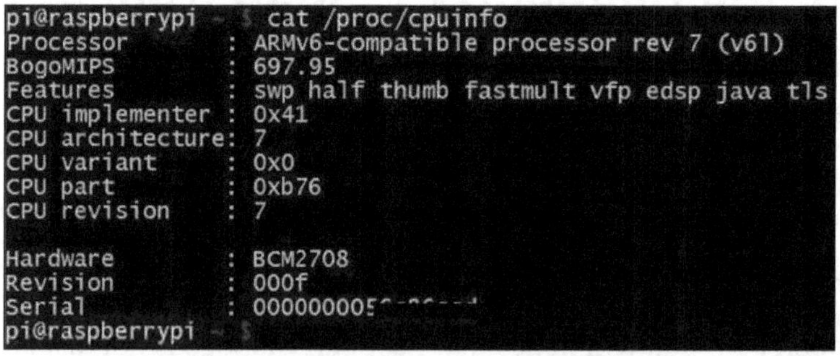

```
pi@raspberrypi - $ cat /proc/cpuinfo
Processor       : ARMv6-compatible processor rev 7 (v6l)
BogoMIPS        : 697.95
Features        : swp half thumb fastmult vfp edsp java tls
CPU implementer : 0x41
CPU architecture: 7
CPU variant     : 0x0
CPU part        : 0xb76
CPU revision    : 7

Hardware        : BCM2708
Revision        : 000f
Serial          : 0000000005
pi@raspberrypi - $
```

Overclock Raspberry Pi without voiding warranty

Go to Raspberry Pi terminal and enter the following command:

```
sudo apt-get update
sudo apt-get install raspberrypi* raspi-config
sudo raspi-config
```

Choose the overclock option as shown in the following screenshot:

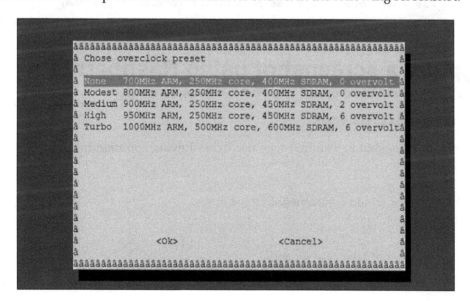

Click on **Finish** and press *Enter*. The result is shown in the following screenshot:

Freeing up RAM on Raspberry Pi

Go to Raspberry Pi terminal and enter the following command:

```
sudosu
free -m(check available memory)
sync
echo 3 > /proc/sys/vm/drop_caches
```

The following command will free RAM (which cleans up page files and other files):

```
free -m ( now check available memory)
```

Set memory split between ARM and GPU in Raspberry Pi

Go to Raspberry Pi terminal and enter the following commands to set memory split between ARM and GPU:

```
Gpu_mem - It sets GPU memory in MB. Defauly 64 Min - 16
Gpu_mem_256 - GPU memory for 256 MB Max.192 (Override gpu_mem)
GPu_mem_512 - GPU memory for 512 MB device . Max. 448 ( Overridegpu_mem)
```

Capture a screenshot using Raspberry Pi

Go to Raspberry Pi terminal and enter the following command:

```
sudo apt-get install scrot
```

To take the screenshot in terminal type use the following command:

```
scrot
```

To take a current window screenshot:

```
scrot -bu
```

To take a screenshot after few seconds:

```
sleep 5; scrot -bu // Take screenshot of focused window after 5 seconds
```

Find the IP address of the Raspberry Pi

As a beginner, you might have trouble finding the IP address of Raspberry Pi. Execute the following command to get the IP address of Raspberry Pi:

```
ifconfig
```

The following screenshot is a result of the preceding code:

If you are using wlan, you will find the IP address under wlan0.

Buy a Raspberry Pi case

ModMyPi has a great range of colorful cases made using state-of-the-art injection molding techniques. Link: `https://www.modmypi.com/shop/raspberry-pi-cases`.

Make your own Raspberry Pi case

You might have heard of Google Cardboard, which is a DIY virtual reality headset made using cardboards. Similarly, you can create your own Raspberry Pi case using this printable PDF. Link: `http://squareitround.co.uk/Resources/Punnet_net_Alpha3.pdf`.

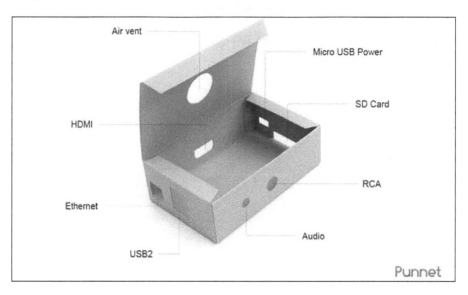

Use Chrome browser in Raspberry Pi

Go to Raspberry Pi terminal and enter the following command:

```
sudo apt- get install chromium-browser
```

This will install the Chromium browser in your Raspberry Pi.

Shut down your Raspberry Pi

Pulling the plug is one of the worst things you can do and it can easily lead to a completely corrupt filesystem. If this happens, you'll lose your files and will need to do a completely fresh install, and there's nothing particularly quick or easy about this. The following commands will shut down Raspberry Pi:

```
sudo shutdown -h 0
sudo shutdown now
```

The following commands will reboot Raspberry Pi:

```
sudo shutdown -r 0
sudo reboot now
```

I would like to connect x device to my Raspberry Pi. How can I be sure it is going to work?

Unless you like the challenge of writing drivers and figuring out why a piece of hardware connected to your computer does not function as it should, before buying any peripherals for your Raspberry Pi, check the list of verified peripherals on the embedded Linux wiki http://elinux.org/RPi_VerifiedPeripherals.

Some useful commands

- `cat` file: This shows the contents of a file
- `echo` "text": This prints text on the screen
- `find` directory (name x): Finds all the named x under a directory
- `grep` text file: This finds text within a file
- `less` file: This shows the contents of a file and allows the user to move up and down through the file

- `ls` directory: This shows a list of files in a directory
- `more` file: This shows the contents of a file and allows the user to move down slowly through the file
- `rm` file: This removes (deletes) a file
- `sort` file: This sorts the contents of a file
- `sudo` command: This runs a command as superuser
- `wc` file: This count the number of lines, words, and characters in a file

Resources for advanced users

Having understood the concepts introduced in this book, you might want to build more advanced projects with your Raspberry Pi. This section has information on some DIY projects as well as some inspirational projects such as building a supercomputer. These projects and some advanced resources will have an idea of what people all over world are building using Raspberry Pi.

Projects

This section contains some of the cool projects that people have built using Raspberry Pi.

The touchscreen car dashboard

If you're prepared to put in some time and effort, you can use Raspberry Pi to create your very own touchscreen car dashboard, something that would cost hundreds of dollars off the shelf. It's powered by the XMBC media center software, so you can play music, watch videos, browse through photos, and more.

Refer to `http://www.instructables.com/id/Raspberry-Pi-Touch-Screen-Car-Computer/` for detailed information.

A talking book player

If you or one of your relatives have trouble scanning text, then this Raspberry Pi-powered device will convert it into speech; but even if you don't have any problems with reading books, it's still a fun project to try. You'll need a few add-on parts and the quality isn't as good as a professionally produced audio book, but it's all about the joy of tinkering.

Refer to `http://www.kolibre.org/en/demo` for detailed information.

The Morse code transmitter

Mix the new and old technologies with your very own Raspberry Pi-powered Morse code station. You will need some extra bits and pieces, plus the wherewithal to program the Raspberry Pi (keyboard, mouse, and monitor), but once it's done you'll have a device that can encode and decode Morse; add a vintage key for extra authenticity.

Refer to `http://www.raspberrypi.org/learning/morse-code/` for detailed information.

The automated pet feeder

David Bryan was going out of town for the weekend and was worried about his cats. It suddenly hit him that he could build an automated cat feeder. David achieved his goal with the help of Raspberry Pi. The project cost him a little less than $150 and only took about 4 to 6 hours to complete. For complete instructions on how to build your own Raspberry Pi-powered pet feeder, refer to `http://drstrangelove.net/2013/12/raspberry-pi-power-cat-feeder-updates/`.

Home automation system using Raspberry Pi and Arduino

Instead of concentrating on simple things such as lights or automated blinds, with the home automation system, you can monitor for water leaks, see if the garage door is open, check for new e-mail, watch for movement, sense for gas, and even see how the dog is doing. The system uses both an Arduino and Raspberry Pi along with a ton of various sensors to monitor the house. You can set up the system to send you alerts when something happens or just monitor everything from your phone.

Refer to `http://www.instructables.com/id/Uber-Home-Automation/` for detailed information.

Face-recognizing safe with Raspberry Pi

Having a safe is a great way to store your valuables, and now you can lock them away in a DIY, face-recognizing setup with a free software, Raspberry Pi, and a Raspberry Pi camera. The free software is based on OpenCV, a small program that runs well on Raspberry Pi, and the camera is just a proper Raspberry Pi camera module. Once everything is set up, you train the installed software to recognize your face and hide your prized possessions away. If you're concerned with thieves printing out a picture of your face, fear not; first of all, they would have to know it's a face-recognizing safe, and second, you can adjust the sensitivity to make the software much stricter.

Refer to `http://makezine.com/projects/make-40/face-recognition-treasure-safe/` for detailed information.

Supercomputer

A single Raspberry Pi is about as powerful as a Pentium 2 with graphics on par with the original XBox. Connect 64 of them together, like one professor from the University of Southampton did, and you have some serious power at your fingertips. Professor Simon Cox put out a tutorial on how to make a 64-node (or more) supercomputer by racking that many Raspberry Pis. One recommended technique is to build your racks from Lego.

Refer to `http://www.southampton.ac.uk/~sjc/raspberrypi/pi_supercomputer_southampton.htm` for detailed information.

Useful resources

Some of the useful resources that will help you build your own projects and solve problems that are not discussed in this book are:

- **The Raspberry Pi website**: On the Raspberry Pi website, you will find all of the news, new projects, builds, and notices for new Raspbian versions. You will also find community news, updates on what the developers are doing, and get access to the online forum. Check out Raspberry Pi's website at `www.raspberrypi.org`.

- **The MagPi magazine**: The MagPi magazine is a free download created by the Raspberry Pi community, for the Raspberry Pi community. Each issue contains a diverse selection of topics, all focused on Raspberry Pi. There are regular articles on programming in Python, Scratch, and C++, plus numerous hardware projects using the GPIO interface. You can read all downloaded issues online at `http://themagpi.com/`. It is also available in print edition. Refer to the MagPi website for subscription.

- **The Reddit website**: Reddit is also a very good place to find news and project ideas—even YouTube videos—of some great Raspberry Pi projects. With a good community, a lot of help and assistance is available via `www.reddit.com/r/raspberry_pi`.

- **The OpenCV website**: *Chapter 5, Introduction to Image Processing* and *Chapter 6, Image Processing Algorithms*, focuses on image processing, and computer vision and fundamental concepts were covered. If you want to go deep in this area, refer to the website of the library (OpenCV) that was used in this book. You will find community news, updates on what the developers are doing, and get access to the online forum. Checkout the OpenCV website at `http://www.opencv.org`.

- **Learning Python**: In this book, the Python language is used to develop all the projects because Python is one of the official languages that is supported on Raspberry Pi. In this book, a basic Python was used, and if you want to learn more about Python refer to `http://learnpythonthehardway.org/` to enrich your knowledge of the Python language.

Summary

This chapter provided solutions to some of the common problems that you faced while working on Raspberry Pi. The second section of the chapter mentioned interesting tips and tricks. The last section of the chapter mentioned a few DIY projects that you might want to pursue with the resources provided.

If you face any issues in any of the projects mentioned in the book or you notice a typo/error in any of the chapters, feel free to mail me at `samarth@outlook.com`.

Index

D

data types, Python 42, 43
decorators, Python 44
digital clock
 init function, adding 91
 clear function, adding 91
 cmd function, adding 92, 93
 developing 82
 HD44780-based LCD, using 83, 84
 LCD pins, connecting 86, 87
 message function, adding 93
 Raspberry Pi GPIO pins, connecting 86, 87
 Raspberry Pi, setting up 83
 requisites 82
 scripting 88, 90
dilation 185
diodes 74
distance calculation, remote-controlled
  robot
 Raspberry Pi pins, connecting 120
 Raspberry Pi, setting up 119
 scripting 121-123
 ultrasonic sensors pins, connecting 120
 ultrasonic sensor used 119

E

edge detection 187, 188
electronic components
 about 71, 106
 breadboard 77, 78
 diodes 74
 integrated circuits (IC) 76
 LCD 77
 level converter 111
 motor driver IC 111
 motors 107
 multimeter 108, 109
 Raspberry Pi battery 117
 Raspberry Pi camera 113
 Raspberry Pi Wi-Fi module 117, 118
 robotic base 110
 resistors 71-74

 sensors 77
 switches 74-76
 symbol 79
 ultrasonic sensor 116
 wire 77
 WiringPi 82
e-mail notifier
 developing 93
 LCD pins, connecting 94
 Raspberry Pi GPIO pins, connecting 94
 scripting 94-98
erosion 184
eye detection 196, 197

F

face detection 193-195
face-recognizing safe, Raspberry Pi
 about 225
 URL 225
filesystem, expanding 11-13
firmware updates, troubleshooting 214
Flask
 about 45-47
 applications, deploying 62, 63
 URL 47
frames per second (FPS) 165

G

grayscale image
 about 145, 146
 image, saving as 155
group of pictures (GOP) value 163

H

H-Bridge
 about 111
 structure diagram 111
home automation system project
 about 225
 URL 225
Honda Asimo
 URL 106

Thank you for buying
Learning Raspberry Pi

About Packt Publishing

Packt, pronounced 'packed', published its first book, *Mastering phpMyAdmin for Effective MySQL Management*, in April 2004, and subsequently continued to specialize in publishing highly focused books on specific technologies and solutions.

Our books and publications share the experiences of your fellow IT professionals in adapting and customizing today's systems, applications, and frameworks. Our solution-based books give you the knowledge and power to customize the software and technologies you're using to get the job done. Packt books are more specific and less general than the IT books you have seen in the past. Our unique business model allows us to bring you more focused information, giving you more of what you need to know, and less of what you don't.

Packt is a modern yet unique publishing company that focuses on producing quality, cutting-edge books for communities of developers, administrators, and newbies alike. For more information, please visit our website at www.packtpub.com.

About Packt Open Source

In 2010, Packt launched two new brands, Packt Open Source and Packt Enterprise, in order to continue its focus on specialization. This book is part of the Packt Open Source brand, home to books published on software built around open source licenses, and offering information to anybody from advanced developers to budding web designers. The Open Source brand also runs Packt's Open Source Royalty Scheme, by which Packt gives a royalty to each open source project about whose software a book is sold.

Writing for Packt

We welcome all inquiries from people who are interested in authoring. Book proposals should be sent to author@packtpub.com. If your book idea is still at an early stage and you would like to discuss it first before writing a formal book proposal, then please contact us; one of our commissioning editors will get in touch with you.

We're not just looking for published authors; if you have strong technical skills but no writing experience, our experienced editors can help you develop a writing career, or simply get some additional reward for your expertise.

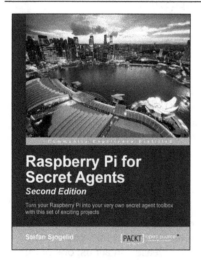

Raspberry Pi Networking Cookbook

ISBN: 978-1-84969-460-5   Paperback: 204 pages

An epic collection of practical and engaging recipes for the Raspberry Pi!

1. Learn how to install, administer, and maintain your Raspberry Pi.

2. Create a network fileserver for sharing documents, music, and videos.

3. Host a web portal, collaboration wiki, or even your own wireless access point.

Raspberry Pi Server Essentials

ISBN: 978-1-78328-469-6   Paperback: 116 pages

Transform your Raspberry Pi into a server for hosting websites, games, or even your Bitcoin network

1. Unlock the various possibilities of using Raspberry Pi as a server.

2. Configure a media center for your home or sharing with friends.

3. Connect to the Bitcoin network and manage your wallet.

Please check **www.PacktPub.com** for information on our titles